Junior Master Gardener Handbook

Level 1

Texas Agricultural Extension Service

The Texas A&M University System

Published by:
Texas Agricultural Extension Service
Agricultural Communications
107 Reed McDonald Building
Texas A&M University
College Station, Texas 77843-2112
http://agpublications.tamu.edu

Copies may be ordered from:
Extension Distribution and Supply
P.O. Box 1209
Bryan, Texas 77806

ISBN 0-9672990-0-4

The terms JMG,^{SM} Junior Master Gardener,^{SM} Golden Ray Series^{SM} and associated logo design are service marks of the Texas Agricultural Extension Service.

A Message for Parents and Leaders

Welcome to the Junior Master Gardener℠ (JMG℠) program. The JMG program is a new and innovative 4-H youth gardening project. It is modeled after the highly popular Master Gardener program, and offers horticulture and environmental science education through fun and creative activities.

Each level of the program is supported by a youth handbook and a leader/teacher guide. Level One is designed for grades 3 through 5.

In this handbook you will find both group and individual activities. Group activities can be done with a school class, JMG club, after-school program, home school group, or any group of interested young gardeners. Individual activities allow young gardeners to learn on their own. Flexibility is a key component in the JMG program. With so many activities to choose from, JMG leaders or individual gardeners can customize the program to meet their own needs and interests.

The JMG program introduces young gardeners to the art and science of gardening, and helps them develop leadership and life skills to become good citizens within their communities, schools and families.

Contact your county Extension agent for more information about becoming involved with Junior Master Gardener℠ and other 4-H activities. The JMG web site *http://juniormastergardener.tamu.edu* also has more information about the program. If there are no JMG activities currently in your community, consider becoming a leader and starting a JMG program for your town, school or neighborhood.

A Message for Future Junior Master Gardeners

As a Junior Master Gardener, you may be new to the 4-H program. There are many ways to be active in the Junior Master Gardener 4-H program. You can join a JMG club or interest group. You can attend camps, or local, district and state 4-H and Junior Master Gardener activities. You can share what you have learned with friends and your community. You will have fun and learn many new things in the JMG program.

The 4-H motto is "To Make the Best Better." As a Junior Master Gardener, you will help make the world a better and more beautiful place.

Using Your Junior Master Gardener Handbook

Your Junior Master Gardener Handbook will help you learn more about the environment and the plant world around you. There are eight exciting chapters in the Handbook. In each chapter you will learn how to do many new things and, most important, you'll have fun. At the end of each chapter there is a page called Leadership/Community Service Projects. These are projects and activities that you can do with your JMG group to share all the many things you have learned with your family, friends and community.

The handbook has places for you to write, draw or circle the activities that you have completed. This is a way for you to keep a record of all the many adventures you have had in the Junior Master Gardener program.

How to Become a Certified Junior Master Gardener?

By doing just one group and one individual activity in each section of each of the eight chapters, you can become a certified Junior Master Gardener. Your group also will choose one leadership/community service project to complete for each chapter. Circle the group activities that your JMG group chooses for each section, and have your leader or parent initial all of the individual activities that you do. This is a great way to show your progress and to share with others all the things that you do in the JMG program!

Your JMG leader/teacher has information about registering your JMG group and getting your certificates from the leader/teacher guide or from the county Extension agent.

Let's Get Growing!

An exciting adventure is just waiting for you in the pages of your Junior Master Gardener Handbook. Make plantable greeting cards. . .discover the wonderful world of worms. . .find out how plants clean water. . . create your own spider web. . .grow your own vegetables. . .make yummy dishes for you and your family. . .and so much more!

So come on and "Get Jammin' with JMG!"

CONTENTS

Chapter 1. Plant Growth and Development. 2

You'll learn how plants grow and make our world a better place.

Chapter 2. Soils and Water. 28

You'll get your hands dirty and learn how soil and water are important to plants and all living things.

Chapter 3. Ecology and Environmental Horticulture 42

You'll get the big picture of how people, plants and animals all depend upon each other and how you can help to take care of our environment.

Chapter 4. Insects and Diseases. 64

You'll find out what's bugging you and your plants by exploring the world of insects and plant diseases.

Chapter 5. Landscape Horticulture 98

You'll learn how to create and take care of beautiful gardens, and how to attract birds, insects and other creatures to your backyard or neighborhood.

Chapter 6. Fruits and Nuts. 124

You'll learn about many different kinds of fruits and nuts, and make fruit smoothies, raisins, and even peanut butter!

Chapter 7. Vegetables and Herbs 138

You'll learn to grow many different kinds of vegetables and herbs and how to cook them in some yummy dishes.

Chapter 8. Life Skills and Career Exploration 158

You'll learn more about you, your friends and your school, and discover how to make plans for your future.

FOREWORD

The Junior Master Gardener program began as a dream of a few avid Master Gardeners, teachers, children and Extension faculty. These few planted the initial seed that has now germinated into a premier children's gardening program. More than 600 children and adults contributed to the development, writing, layout, art and piloting of this curriculum, and have shaped and molded this program into a handbook and teacher/leader guide that will be fun, educational and exciting for everyone! Many of these individuals are listed in the Appendix beginning on page 183. Our hope is that the Junior Master Gardener program will use horticulture as a tool for cultivating children and communities.

Bloom Where You Are Planted and Happy Gardening!

Lisa A. Whittlesey
State Junior Master Gardener Coordinator

Randy L. Seagraves
Junior Master Gardener Curriculum
Coordinator

Plant Growth and Development

Importance and Uses of Plants

Have you ever imagined what our world would be like without plants? Plants are the beginning of the food chain. Both animals and people eat plants. Plants also make our world beautiful. Trees give shade during the summer and protect us from the wind in winter. Shrubs, vines and flowers make our homes pretty and provide a place to live for wildlife such as birds, squirrels and insects.

Look at the clothes in your closet. Did you know that some clothes are made from plants, or that our ancestors used plants to dye their clothing? Long ago, if people were sick they didn't go to the pharmacy or grocery store for medicine. They used plants to treat common illnesses.

When we breathe, we are taking oxygen into our bodies. Plants make the oxygen that we breathe. Without plants we would not be able to live.

Let's learn more about what plants do for us.

THINGS FOR YOUR JMG GROUP TO DO:

- ❀ Hamburger Plant
- ❀ Benefits Mobile
- ❀ Know & Show Sombrero
- ❀ The Medicine Plant
- ❀ The Choo-Choo Song (see Rhythms section)

THINGS FOR YOU TO DO:

❀ Plant Product Collage

Clip pictures from magazines and newspapers that show products that come from plants, such as furniture, clothes, food and houses. Arrange these pictures on poster board to make an art collage.

_____ date completed

_____ leader/parent initials

❀ Plant Press Sandwich

A plant press removes water from plants so that they will last a very long time. Select a variety of plant leaves and flowers to press. It is best to collect plants in the afternoon when they are dry. Thinner leaves and flowers work best for pressing. Collect plant parts of different shapes, colors and sizes. To make a plant press sandwich, cut two pieces of cardboard about the size of a piece of notebook paper. Cut several sheets of newspaper the same size. Lay two or three sheets of newspaper on one piece of cardboard. On top of this lay a few sheets of paper towel. Arrange flowers or leaves on the paper towel. Lay a few more sheets  of paper towel on top of plants, and several more layers of newspaper on the stack. Cover the stack with the second piece of cardboard to make a sandwich. Tie the sandwich tightly together with string, or stack heavy books on top to press the layers. Keep the press closed for several days. When plants are pressed you can gently brush glue on the back of a plant and glue it to colored paper to make a card for someone.

_____ date completed

_____ leader/parent initials

🌼 **Journal**

In the space below, tell what you know about why plants are so important.

_____

_____

_____

_____

_____

_____

_____

_____

_____ date completed

_____ leader/parent initials

Plant Classification

There are millions of plants in the world. Can you imagine how hard it would be to identify all of them? If you took all the clothes from your room and threw them on the floor, it would be hard to find anything. But if you organize your clothes so that socks are together, shirts are together, and pants are together, it is easy to find the clothes you want.

Scientists have ways of organizing plants. They look at different plant parts such as flowers, leaves, stems and fruits, and group plants that are similar. For example, some plants produce flowers, while others produce cones. Plants are also grouped according to where and how they grow. Some plants, such as trees, live for many years. Other plants, such as radishes, live for only one season before they die. Go outside and see all the many different plants in your neighborhood. Take a minute to look closely at one plant and imagine what other plants might be related to it. Let's explore the world of plant classification.

THINGS FOR YOUR JMG GROUP TO DO:

🌼 Leaf-and-Seed-Sort Information Chart

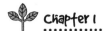

THINGS FOR YOU TO DO:

✿ Leaf Rubbing Rainbow

Find several leaves of different shapes and sizes. Collect both **monocot** and **dicot** leaves. Place a leaf under a piece of paper. Remove the paper from a crayon and use the wide edge of the crayon to rub over the leaf. Use another leaf and another crayon to rub a new leaf pattern on the paper. Continue rubbing leaves on the page until you have created a pattern you like.

What's a monocot?
✔ Has only one seed leaf.
✔ Has parallel veins.

What's a dicot?
✔ Has two seed leaves.
✔ Has netted veins.

_____date completed
_____leader/parent initials

✿ Can You Be-Leaf It?

People who study plants can identify them by their leaf edges. Find six different leaves and sketch their edges in the boxes below.

Leaves come in lots of shapes and sizes. Here are some examples of common leaf edges that you might find.

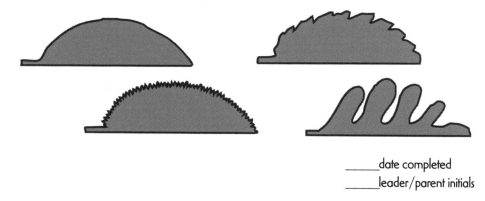

_____ date completed
_____ leader/parent initials

※ **JMG Web**

Go to: *http://juniormastergardener.tamu.edu* and click on Plant Growth and Development. Choose one of the activities under Classification and complete it.

_____ date completed
_____ leader/parent initials

Plant Parts

A plant has many different parts. The plant's body parts work together just as your body parts work together. The plant roots are found in the soil. They carry water and nutrients to the plant. The stem supports the plant and carries water and food throughout the plant. Leaves use sunlight to make food for the plant. Flowers are usually the bright and colorful part of the plant. When flowers are pollinated by insects or wind they produce seeds that are stored in fruit. Wow! Plants are really amazing.

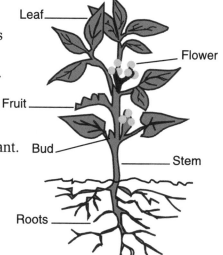

THINGS FOR YOUR JMG GROUP TO DO:

※ Plant Parts Rap
※ Touch and Tell
※ Plant Parts We Eat
※ Seed Science
※ Flower Dissection

THINGS FOR YOU TO DO:

❀ **Fantastical Plants**

Create your own plant using things you find around your home, such as straw, buttons, string, balloons, or anything else you can find. Be sure your fantastical plant has roots, stems, leaves, flowers, fruit and seeds.

_____ date completed
_____ leader/parent initials

❀ **JMG Rap Performance**

Find the rap song in the Rhythms section of your handbook. Perform the Plant Parts Rap for a family member, friend, JMG group or class.

_____ date completed
_____ leader/parent initials

❀ **Uncover and Discover**

There are two kinds of plant roots—**taproots** and **fibrous** roots. Go to your backyard, school ground, or neighborhood and carefully pull up six different plants. See whether they have taproots or fibrous roots. (Note: Be a good Junior Master Gardener and ask before you pick!)

Fibrous root of grass

Taproot of carrot

_____ date completed
_____ leader/parent initials

Did you know that you can tell how old trees are by examining the inside of a stem? Find a piece of cut firewood or the stump of a tree that has recently been cut. You will see rings. These are growth rings made by special plant cells called **xylem.** These cells carry the water and nutrients to the top of the tree.

Each year a tree makes a new ring. By counting the rings you can find out the age of the tree. The width of the rings can also tell you if the plant had a good or bad year. Wider rings mean that the tree received lots of water that year. How old is the tree you found?

Look at the tree rings in this picture and answer these questions:

How old is the tree? _____

How many good (or wet) years did it have? _____

_____ date completed
_____ leader/parent initials

Plant Needs

People need air, water, food, clothing and shelter to live. Did you know that plants have special needs, too? Plants need water, air and food to live. Beyond these basic needs, different plants have different needs. Some plants require more care than others. For example, some plants like to grow in a desert. If you know a plant's special needs you will be able to grow and care for that plant.

THINGS FOR YOUR JMG GROUP TO DO:
❀ P.L.A.N.T. Needs
❀ What's Not the Same?
❀ Plant People
❀ Picture Yourself a Plant

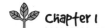
THINGS FOR YOU TO DO:

❀ Variable Menu

You have learned that plants have many needs. Now you will be a scientist to learn how plants grow best. You may do an experiment to test how plants grow with different kinds of soil, or how they grow with different types of water.

Find three containers that are alike. You can use paper cups, milk cartons or small pots. Be sure to poke a small hole in the bottom of each container for drainage if it doesn't already have one. Fill out the Variable Menu Lab Report on page 11 as you do the experiment.

Soil Variable: Fill each container with a different kind of soil. You could use sand, gravel, potting soil, dirt from your yard, or any other type of soil. Make sure you put the same amount in each container. Plant three bean seeds in each container and give each the same amount of water. Put the containers in the same place so they all get the same amount of light.

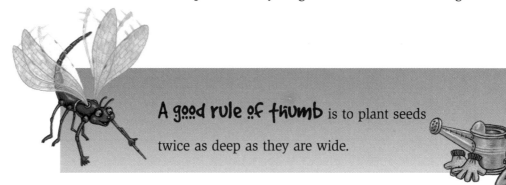

A good rule of thumb is to plant seeds twice as deep as they are wide.

Water Variable: Fill each of three containers with the same kind and amount of soil. Plant three bean seeds in each container and place them in the same location where they will get the same amount of light. Water each container with a different type of water. You can use tap water, rainwater, very salty water, bottled drinking water, or your own idea. Use the same amount of water on each plant. Keep the soil slightly moist.

Variable Menu Lab Report

1. What variable are you using in your experiment? _____

2. Write what variable is in each container in the blanks below:

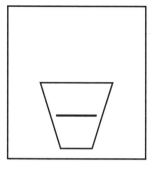 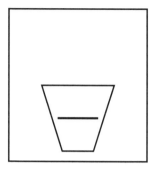 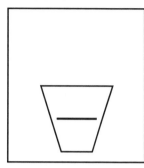

3. Which variable do you think will help the plant grow best?

_____

4. Which variable do you think will make the plant grow poorly?

_____

5. Let the plants grow for 2 weeks. Draw what each plant looks like in the boxes above.

_____ date completed
_____ leader/parent initials

❧ 2-liter Terrarium

A terrarium is a special container that keeps plants warm and moist. You can make a terrarium from a 2-liter soda bottle. Have an adult help you cut off the spout end of the bottle about 4 inches from the top. Fill the bottom part of the bottle with soil. Plant seeds (such as radish, ryegrass or leaf lettuce) or a small plant, and water until the soil is slightly damp. Turn the spout end upside down and set it in the bottle. Grow the plant for at least 4 weeks. Write what you see happening each week on the next page.

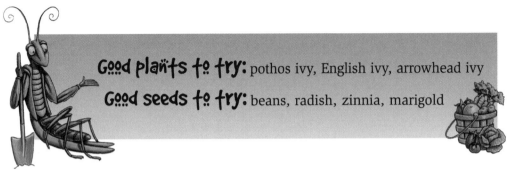

Good plants to try: pothos ivy, English ivy, arrowhead ivy

Good seeds to try: beans, radish, zinnia, marigold

First Week _____

Second Week _____

Third Week _____

Fourth Week _____

_____ date completed
_____ leader/parent initials

Plant Growth

You have learned that plants have special needs just as people do. When plants receive the proper light, water and nutrients, they grow and thrive. Most plants start as seeds and develop during their life cycles. Let's take a look at how plants grow.

THINGS FOR YOUR JMG GROUP TO DO:
- Coconut Float
- Plant Performance
- Topiary Design
- Power Seeds

THINGS FOR YOU TO DO:
- **Pinwheel Plants**

  Cut four pieces of white construction paper 3 inches high and 5 inches wide (or use index cards). On the first card draw a picture of a seed sprouting. On

the second card draw the same plant forming leaves. Draw pictures of the plant growing larger on the next card. On the fourth card draw the plant with a flower. Glue or tape the backs of the cards together as shown in the picture on page 12, leaving a small space in the middle for a pencil.

Glue the pencil in place. Twirl the pencil and watch the plant grow!

Create one more pinwheel of your own that shows how to plant a seed, a plant growing a flower, or your own idea.

_____ date completed

_____ leader/parent initials

❀ Pinto Plant Parts

For this activity you will need 25 containers. You may use paper cups, milk cartons or small paper pots that you make. To make a paper pot, tear a long strip of newspaper that is about 5 inches wide. Find an empty paper towel tube. Roll the strip of newspaper tightly around one end of the cardboard tube, leaving about 1 inch of paper off the end of the tube. Fold the loose edge of the paper over the end of the tube to make a bottom. Slip the paper pot off the tube and fill it with soil.

Plant a bean seed in each pot. Keep them moist until they begin to sprout. Once a day, carefully pull one of the growing sprouts out of the soil and rinse it off. Look closely to see how the roots, stem or leaves have grown. Staple 26 sheets of paper together to make a booklet. On the front page write the title "Plant Growth." Each day that you examine a bean seed, draw a sketch of it on a new page until your booklet is filled.

_____ date completed

_____ leader/parent initials

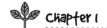

❀ Seed Sock Search

You have learned that seeds travel away from their mother plant so they don't have to compete for water, light or other plant needs. Put a large sock on over one shoe. Take a walk outside in your yard, neighborhood, park, in the woods, or school ground. Then remove the sock and see how many different seeds are attached to it. You will find more seeds if you do this activity during the warm season. Plant your sock in an open place in your yard, or in a pot. Count how many seedlings come up from your seedy sock.

_____ date completed
_____ leader/parent initials

❀ See the Seed Flee

Using these pictures, find four seeds that travel four different ways. Remember that many seeds can be spread in more than one way.

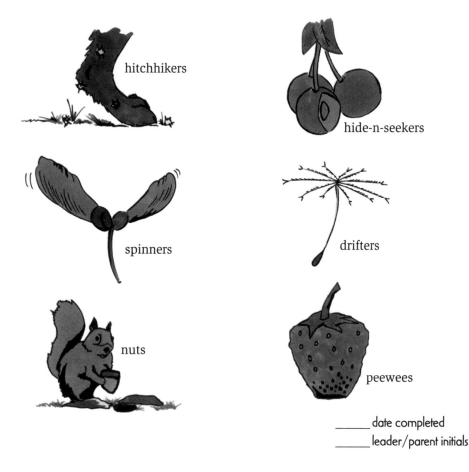

hitchhikers

hide-n-seekers

spinners

drifters

nuts

peewees

_____ date completed
_____ leader/parent initials

Plant Processes

Have you ever wondered why plants like to grow in the sun? Plants need sunlight to make food. Plants make their own food in a process called **photosynthesis.** Photosynthesis happens mainly in leaves. Plants combine carbon dioxide from the air, green pigment (**chlorophyll**) from the leaves, and sunlight to produce food. When plants make their own food through photosynthesis they give off oxygen. People need oxygen to breathe. Isn't it amazing how plants and people depend on each other!

When people work hard, they lose water through their skin. This is called sweat or perspiration. Plants lose water through their leaves. This process is called **transpiration.** Water from plants escapes into the air and is part of the water cycle. Just think. . .the tree in your yard could be providing water for rain in another part of the world. Let's have fun looking at how plants work.

THINGS FOR YOUR JMG GROUP TO DO:
- ❀ Oxygen Factory
- ❀ Gas Gobblers
- ❀ Spinning Seeds

THINGS FOR YOU TO DO:
- ❀ **Initial Leaves**

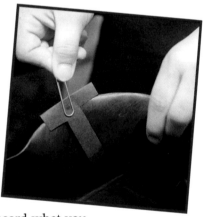

    Fold a piece of dark construction paper into a small rectangle about 1 inch by 2 inches. Cut the initial of your first name out of the paper, leaving some of the fold uncut. When you open the paper you should have two initials in a mirror image. Slip the paper over a large plant leaf in your yard. The fold side will be on the edge of the leaf. Use tape or a paper clip to secure the other side. Leave your letter on the leaf for 2 weeks. Remove the leaf and record what you see. Why do you think this happened? Show your answer to your group leader.

_____

_____

_____ date completed
_____ leader/parent initials

❋ Plant Maze

One really interesting thing about plants is that they are **phototropic.** That means they will bend toward light. Try building this plant maze to see how they do it.

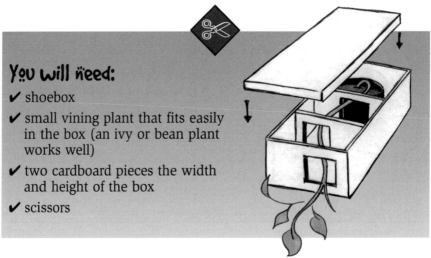

You will need:

✔ shoebox
✔ small vining plant that fits easily in the box (an ivy or bean plant works well)
✔ two cardboard pieces the width and height of the box
✔ scissors

Cut a square in one end of the box. Cut a square in each piece of cardboard, at a different place on each piece. Place your plant in one end of the box, and space the cardboard pieces in the box. Put the lid on the box. The plant will grow through the maze to the hole at the other end of the box. Draw a picture of what your plant maze looks like and how the plant grew.

_____ date completed
_____ leader/parent initials

❀ Upside Down Seed

Have you ever planted a seed upside down? With this experiment you can find out which way a seed should be planted. Poke a hole in the bottoms of six paper cups and fill them with soil. In each cup plant a seed pointing a different direction. Sunflower seeds work best, but you may use bean seeds.

On the outside of the cup draw the direction the seed is pointing. Keep the soil moist until the plants sprout. Scientists make predictions about what will happen in an experiment. What do you think will happen?

_____

_____

_____

_____ date completed

_____ leader/parent initials

❀ Patriotic Plant

Have an adult help you split a celery stalk or the stem of a white carnation into three sections. Put each section of the stem into a container of water. Add a few drops of red food coloring to one container, blue food coloring to another, and no food coloring to the third. Watch for 2 days and see how the plant pulls the water through its stem. Take a picture or draw a picture of your experiment and share it with others.

_____ date completed

_____ leader/parent initials

❀ Smothering Stomata

You know that plants take in air through little holes called **stomata** on the bottom sides of their leaves. What do you think would happen if you blocked all the stomata on a leaf? Rub petroleum jelly, shortening or oil on the underside of a plant leaf. Make sure you apply a thin coat to the entire underside. What do you think will happen?

_____

Check the plant after 1 day, 3 days and 1 week. What happened to the plant after 1 day?

_____

_____

What happened to the plant after 3 days?

_____

_____

What happened to the plant after 1 week?

_____

_____

_____ date completed
_____ leader/parent initials

Propagation

Propagation means making new plants from older ones. Most plants make new plants by producing seed. Seeds need water, oxygen and the right temperature in order to start growing. Some seeds will germinate and form new plants very quickly. Other seeds take a long time to form new plants.

For some plants it is easier to start new ones by cutting off part of the parent plant. You can use the stem, leaf and roots to start new plants. These pieces are called **cuttings.** Cuttings need to have plenty of moisture in order to form new roots. It is a lot faster to start a new plant from a cutting.

Let's practice starting new plants.

THINGS FOR YOUR JMG GROUP TO DO:
- ❀ Paper Pots
- ❀ Gallon Greenhouse
- ❀ Propagation Demonstration

THINGS FOR YOU TO DO:
- ❀ **Stick and Grow**

    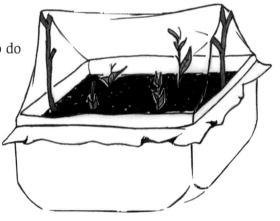

    It is fun to start new plants from cuttings. There are several ways to do it. Be sure to use a sharp knife or pruning shears to make your cuttings. You can make a special container to help your cuttings grow. It is called a gallon greenhouse. To make one, have an adult cut the bottom off a plastic gallon jug. Fill the bottom with potting soil and put your cuttings in it. Be sure the bottoms of the cuttings are buried in the soil. Cover your greenhouse with a piece of plastic wrap. Keep your cuttings moist. Choose four different ways to start new plants and start some of your own.

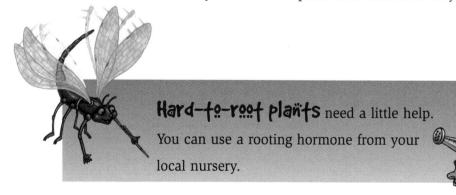

Hard-to-root plants need a little help. You can use a rooting hormone from your local nursery.

Stem Cuttings

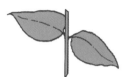

Single eye   Double eye
(The **eye** is the point where the **petiole** attaches to the stem.)

Leaf Cuttings

Leaf with split vein   Leaf with petiole   Leaf section or square
(The **petiole** is the small stalk that attaches the leaf to the stem.)

Root Cuttings

 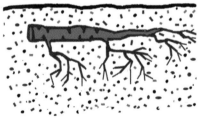

Plant with small roots

Plant with large roots

 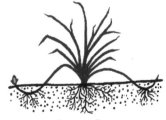

Root division   Layering

Plants to try

Stem

ficus, pothos ivy,
English ivy, geranium,
arrowhead ivy

Leaf

African violet, kalanchoe, begonia

Root

carrot, blackberry

Division
aloe vera,
Mother-in-Law's tongue,
liriope, day lily

Layering
pothos ivy, philodendron,
rubber plant, blackberry

List the types of cuttings you did:

	Type of cutting	Type of plant	How long did it take to root?
1.			
2.			
3.			
4.			

Once your cuttings grow roots, you can put them in another container. Be sure that your container has drain holes in the bottom. Give one of your new plants to a special friend.

_____ date completed
_____ leader/parent initials

❀ Seed Sponges

Find three jars. Fill each halfway full with bean seeds. Fill two of the jars with water to the level of the beans. Put a lid on one of the jars with water.

Observe what happens over 1 week. What happened differently in each jar?

_____

_____

_____

_____

Count how many seeds sprouted in each jar and write the numbers below:

open, dry jar _____

open, wet jar _____

closed, wet jar _____

Which jar had the most sprouted seeds? _____

Why do you think the other two did not have as many sprout?

_____

_____

_____ date completed
_____ leader/parent initials

❊ Time to Transplant

When you germinate a seed in a container, the seedling will soon need to be transplanted to a larger container or outdoors. How do you know when it is time to transplant it? Look at the pictures below and circle the plant with a second pair of leaves.

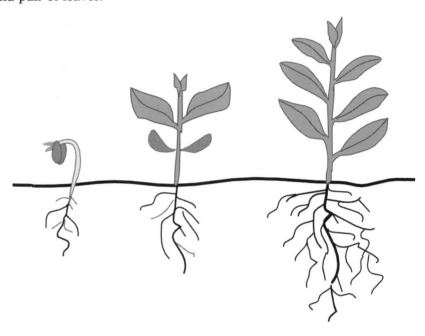

A plant's second pair of leaves are called the **true leaves.** When the true leaves appear it is time to transplant.

Find an egg carton and poke a hole in the bottom of each egg holder. Fill with soil. Plant seeds in each holder. If it is spring, try planting tomatoes, peppers or zinnias. If it is summer, try okra, zinnias or periwinkle. If it is winter, try planting lettuce, spinach or pansies.

Keep the egg carton planter in a sunny place and keep the soil moist.

How many days did it take for the seeds to germinate? _____

How many days did it take for the true leaves to appear? _____

_____ date completed
_____ leader/parent initials

✿ Grow Your Own Pineapple

Go with an adult to the store and buy a pineapple. Cut off the top of the pineapple about 1 inch below the cluster of leaves. You can use this part to start a new pineapple plant. Allow it to dry for several days and then plant it in a large container. The soil level should be at the base of the leaves.

Remove the outside portion of the rest of the pineapple and enjoy eating the delicious fruit. Once your pineapple has rooted, it makes a unique plant.

You can get your pineapple to make a pineapple fruit if you are patient. After about 1 year, the pineapple will be big enough to produce a fruit. It produces the fruit from a flower. If your pineapple has not formed a flower, try this trick. Put an apple next to the plant and put a clear plastic bag over it. Leave it covered for a couple of days. The apple gives off a gas called **ethylene** that helps the pineapple plant bloom. The fruit forms out of the middle of the plant. It is ready to eat when it is a deep golden color.

_____ date completed
_____ leader/parent initials

✿ JMG Web

Go to: *http://juniormastergardener.tamu.edu* and click on Plant Growth and Development. Choose one of the activities under Propagation.

_____ date completed
_____ leader/parent initials

❧ Journal

In the lines below, tell about two different ways to propagate plants.

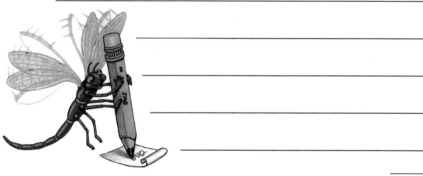

_____

_____

_____

_____

_____

_____

_____

_____

_____

_____

_____ date completed
_____ leader/parent initials

LEADERSHIP/COMMUNITY SERVICE PROJECTS

Your group will choose at least one of the following activities to complete.

❧ Gifts for Others

Dry plants and flowers and create bookmarks or note cards. Take them as gifts to a hospital or nursing home. Or, give them to volunteers at your school or to JMG volunteers.

❧ Variable Day Demonstration

Each person in your JMG group will pick a variable for testing plant growth. It must be something you have not already experimented with. Be creative. You could test freezing seeds, colored light, how plants grow with music–anything you want! Have a special day to show your experiment to the rest of the group.

❧ Adopt-a-Spot

Work with your JMG group to create a large topiary for the entrance of your school.

❧ Share What You Know

Teach one of the activities you did in this section to a group of younger children.

❧ JMG Know & Show Sombrero Competition

Have a competition and choose the most artistic newspaper hats created at the beginning of this section.

❧ Create Your Own

Your JMG group can have fun creating your own unique leadership/community service project.

Circle the project you have completed.

_____ date completed
_____ leader/parent initials

Soils and Water

Soil Color, Texture and Structure

What do beetles, sunflowers, cows and you have in common? Well, all of these things depend on soil to live. Beetles burrow and live in the soil. Sunflowers and other plants grow in soil. The soil anchors the plant and holds water and nutrients that the plant needs to grow. Cows and other animals feed on plants that are growing in soil. Yes, even you depend on soil for the food you eat, the jeans you wear, wood to build houses, and even for sweet treats such as ice cream and chewing gum. Soil is needed for all of these great things we enjoy.

Soil is the building block for all life. Soil is composed of many materials, just like ingredients in your favorite cookie recipe. The main ingredient in soil is rock that has been broken into tiny particles over time. The next soil ingredient is decomposing animals and plants such as the leaves that have fallen in your yard or grass clippings left after mowing. These are broken down by another soil ingredient—**microorganisms.** Microorganisms are creatures that live in the soil. They are too small to see without a microscope. Finally, water and nutrients make the soil recipe complete.

Let's take a closer look at what is found in soil.

THINGS FOR YOUR JMG GROUP TO DO:

- ❋ Touchy Feely
- ❋ Mud Pies
- ❋ Shake, Rattle and Roll
- ❋ Candy Aggregate

THINGS FOR YOU TO DO:

- ❋ **Making a List**

    Soil is full of all sorts of things. Take a handful of soil from the ground and spread it out on a piece of white paper. Look carefully at the soil. If you have one, use a magnifying glass to examine the soil up close. Look for the items on the list below. Put a check beside each item that you find.

    ○ sand   helps the soil to drain

    ○ clay   helps the soil hold water and nutrients

    ○ rocks   turn into sand, silt and clay after a long time

    ○ twigs   when they turn to organic matter they add nutrients and help soils drain

    ○ bits of plants   when they turn to organic matter they add nutrients and help soils drain

    ○ earthworms   help make organic matter and make tunnels that help roots get water and air

    ○ live insects   some insects help plants and some hurt them

    ○ dead insects   when they turn to organic matter they add nutrients and help soils drain

    ○ trash   some trash, such as paper and food scraps, turns to organic matter

    ○ water   when soil is damp roots take water to the rest of the plant

    _____ date completed

    _____ leader/parent initials

❀ Soil Rainbow

Soils can be very different from one place to the next. Soils can be made up of different materials and be different colors. Find at least six sealable plastic bags and go on a soil hunt. Fill each bag with soil from a different place around your neighborhood. Each sample you take should have a different color.

Put a label on each bag and write where the soil came from. When you have filled your bags show them to your group leader.

_____date completed
_____leader/parent initials

❀ Soil Sample

There are laboratories that can study your soil samples for you. Contact your county Extension agent to find out how to take a soil sample from your garden or landscape and get it tested. The phone number for your county Extension agent is in your telephone book under the name of your county. For example, if you live in Brazos County then look in the telephone book under Brazos County. The number may be listed as county Extension office or Cooperative Extension Service. The people in this office will tell you how to take a sample and where to send it to be tested. Most Extension offices will mail your sample for you and will explain the results. The agent can help you decide if you need to add organic matter or fertilizer, and even what plants would do best in your soil.

Call your county Extension office and ask the following questions:
Can you send me information on how to collect a soil sample? _____

How much does it cost to have a soil sample tested? _____

How long does it take to get back results from the laboratory? _____

_____date completed
_____leader/parent initials

❀ Compaction Measurement

Soil should have air spaces in it for plants to grow well. The spaces let water and air move through the soil. Soil that is compacted has been pressed together so the soil does not have many air spaces and has become hard for plants to grow in. Find two empty cans. Fill them with soil from your yard.

Measure how many inches of soil it takes to fill up a can. Use your fist to push the soil down hard in one can. Now measure how many inches of soil you have in that can. Fill in the blanks below.

There were _____ inches of soil in the first can.

There were _____ inches of soil in the can with compacted soil.

Subtract the two numbers above to find the difference between the two cans of soil. The difference between the two cans of soil is _____ inches.

Plants do not grow well in soil that has been compacted because there are no air spaces for water and air to flow through. Find a place outside where the ground is so hard and compacted that nothing is growing there. Write what you think has caused the ground to be compacted.

_____

_____

_____ date completed
_____ leader/parent initials

✻ **JMG Web**
Go to: *http://juniormastergardener.tamu.edu* and click on Soils & Water.
Choose one of the activities under Properties of Soil and complete it.

_____date completed
_____leader/parent initials

Nutrients

We all need certain nutrients to keep our bodies healthy. We get nutrients from eating nutritious foods such as carrots, bananas, beans and cheese. You can also get more of the nutrients you need from vitamins. Just like us, plants need nutrients to stay healthy. Garden plants get nutrients from the soil and from fertilizer we give them.

THINGS FOR YOUR JMG GROUP TO DO:
   ✻ Nutrient Variable
   ✻ The Numbers on the Bag (see Rhythms section)
   ✻ Bumps Below

Soil Improvement

Have you have ever seen leaves falling from the trees? Why do you think the leaves don't just pile up under the trees year after year? Where do the leaves go? The leaves don't pile up because when they die they start to fall apart or decompose. When leaves decompose, they are not leaves any more. They become a part of the soil called **organic matter.** Organic matter is made up of bits and pieces of plants or animals that used to be alive. Organic matter is good for the soil because it helps make the soil more loose so plant roots can grow. Organic matter also helps soil hold water.

THINGS FOR YOUR JMG GROUP TO DO:
   ✻ Building Bins and Compost Sandwiches
   ✻ Composting Critter Page
   ✻ Compost Sandwich Composition

THINGS FOR YOU TO DO:

❀ Planting Trash

Nature recycles everything, even plants and animals. When a plant dies, it falls to the ground and the bacteria and other creatures in the soil turn it into compost. Dig five holes about 6 inches deep. Find five different pieces of trash from the list below. Bury a different piece of trash in each hole. Wait 3 to 4 weeks and dig up the trash. Does it look any different? Can you see any small animals around the place where you buried the trash or in the hole? What do they look like? Put a star beside each item that is turning to compost. Circle the items that did not compost.

soda can
a vegetable scrap
coat hanger
a ball of newspaper
egg shells
plastic bottle
pieces of bread

paper cup
piece of Styrofoam
a rock
food leftovers from your lunch
nonfood leftovers from
  your lunch
a glass jar

_____date completed
_____leader/parent initials

❀ Pile It Up

You learned about how to make and use a compost bin with your JMG group. Now start a compost pile at home. Find a spot that is not in the way and begin to pile up leaves, grass clippings, even a few food scraps every now and then. Be sure to sprinkle a layer of soil over the pile and spray water on it now and then. Perhaps a parent can help you build a bin to hold your compost.

_____date completed
_____leader/parent initials

❀ Journal

In the lines below tell at least three reasons why you think it is important to compost.

_____

_____

_____

_____

_____

_____

_____

_____date completed

_____leader/parent initials

❀ JMGWeb

Go to: *http://juniormastergardener.tamu.edu* and click on Soils and Water. Choose one of the activities under Soil Improvement to complete.

_____date completed

_____leader/parent initials

Water Cycle and You

Did you know that the water you used to brush your teeth this morning may have been some of the same water that rained on your great-great-grandparents' heads, or that dinosaurs drank millions of years ago? The earth is sometimes called the water planet because most of the planet is covered with water. That is good for us, because all living things need water to live.

?

Why do you think we have not used up all of the water yet?

✔ All of the water on the earth now is the same water we have always had.

✔ We have used it over and over again because of the water cycle.

There is liquid water that flows and sloshes in oceans, lakes and rivers. There is solid water (that's ice!) that is in the coldest parts of the world in ice caps and icebergs. There is also invisible gas water called **water vapor** (that's **humidity**) that floats around in the air.

The water rains down on the earth. Some of it soaks deep into the ground and may enter underground rivers called **aquifers.** We can drill wells and get water from aquifers for drinking and watering crops. Some rain falls on the ground and flows into lakes, rivers and oceans. Some of this water evaporates and floats back into the air as water vapor. The water vapor changes to water droplets that make clouds. Rain falls from the clouds back down to earth. This is called the **water cycle.**

THINGS FOR YOUR JMG GROUP TO DO:
- ❧ Earth Apple
- ❧ Cloud Maker
- ❧ The Cycle Song (see Rhythms section)
- ❧ Apple Rings and Banana Chips

THINGS FOR YOU TO DO:
- ❧ **Water Cycle**

The water cycle provides all living things with the clean water they need to live and grow. Each part of the water cycle has a special name. Read the meaning for each word and fill in the boxes on the next page to complete the water cycle.

When rain, sleet, hail or snow falls from the sky it is called **precipitation.**

When the water on land flows to other places it is called **run-off.**

When water changes to water vapor and floats into the air it is called **evaporation.**

When plants change the water in their leaves to water vapor it is called **transpiration.**

When water vapor changes into water drops it is called **condensation.**

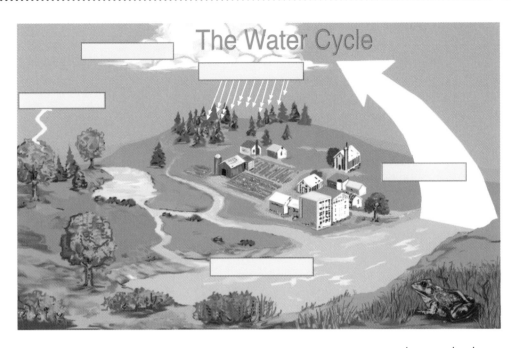

The Water Cycle

_____date completed
_____leader/parent initials

❀ Transpiration Trap

Roots take the water from the ground and leaves put the water back into the air. This is called **transpiration.** You can demonstrate this by tying a clear plastic bag over a small group of leaves on a tree or bush. Use a piece of string to tie the opening of the bag around the stem. Check in a few hours to see the water drops in the bag.

_____date completed
_____leader/parent initials

JMG Trivia: On a hot summer day, a willow tree can lose up to 5,000 gallons of water through its leaves.

❧ How Watery Are You?

It might surprise you to know how much of your body is made up of water. Complete the blanks to find out how many pounds of water are in your body!

Weigh yourself on a scale to find your weight.

I weigh _____ pounds.

Multiply your weight by 2.

_____ pounds x 2 = _____

Divide that number by 3.

_____ ÷ 3 = _____

This is how many pounds of water are in your body.

_____date completed
_____leader/parent initials

Water Movement

When rain falls on the ground, some of it runs off the top and some of it soaks into the soil. When rain runs off the soil and carries soil particles with it, that is called **erosion**. Rainwater going into the soil is called **infiltration**. Water going deeper into the soil is called **percolation**. Plants need water to soak deep into the soil where their roots are. Good soil is loose, with small spaces that allow water to infiltrate and percolate. Water that does not go into the soil cannot get to the roots of a plant.

THINGS FOR YOUR JMG GROUP TO DO:

❧ Out of the Spout
❧ Where Did It Go?
❧ Water Flows, Soil Goes

THINGS FOR YOU TO DO:

❀ Power Shower

Soil that has nothing growing in it will probably wash away when it rains. When soil washes away, it is called **water erosion.** Go outside and find an area on the ground that is just bare soil. Use a 2-liter bottle to pour water onto the soil. Watch how the dirt moves and splashes and the water becomes muddy. Also pour water onto an area of ground where grass is growing. Which area shows more water erosion?

_____date completed

_____leader/parent initials

❀ Water Works

Rainwater sprinkles plants from above. When you water your plant you can water it many different ways. Using a water sprinkler is not the best way to water some plants. One reason is that it is not good for a plant's leaves to be wet very often because they can become sick. Wet leaves also can be damaged by the sun.

Watering plants is called **irrigation.** For the roots to get water, the water must soak several inches into the soil. Try these three types of irrigation and write down which one you think is best. Find three small spots of bare soil. Choose a day when the soil is dry.

l. Overhead Sprinkling

Spray the first spot with a water hose until the ground is completely wet. Poke your finger into the soil in ten different places to see how deep the water soaked into the soil.

2. Flood Irrigation

Use your hand or a shovel to dig a little ditch in the ground that is about 5 inches deep and 2 feet long. Use your hose to fill the little ditch with water. Allow water to soak in. Poke your finger into the soil in ten different places to see how deep the water soaked into the soil.

3. Slow Drip Irrigation

Use a nail to poke a small hole in the bottom of a coffee can. Fill the can with water and place the can on the soil. Wait until the can is empty. Remove the can and poke your finger into the soil in ten different places to see how deep the water soaked into the soil.

Which type of irrigation let water soak in the deepest?

_____

Which type of irrigation let the water spread out the farthest?

_____

_____date completed
_____leader/parent initials

❀ Rain Gauge

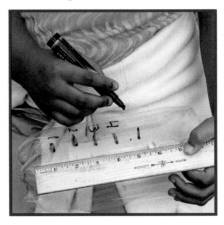

Water is so important to plants that it is good to know how much water your plants are getting. You can make a rain gauge that will tell you how many inches of water have come to your garden. Find a 2-liter bottle that has a flat bottom. Have an adult help you cut the spout off the bottle. Stand a ruler along the side of your bottle. Make a small line on the bottle beside every inch mark on your ruler. You will need a permanent marker to do this.

Number each mark starting at the bottom. Place your rain gauge in your yard or garden. Make sure it is not under the edge of a roof or fence where water might run off into your rain gauge. You might need to put rocks around it to keep it from falling over. Next time it rains, measure the amount of rain in the container.

_____date completed
_____leader/parent initials

LEADERSHIP/COMMUNITY SERVICE ACTIVITIES

Your group will choose one of the following activities to complete.

❀ Help Make Their Bed

Find a flower bed or garden in your community. It could be at your school, at a retirement home, city library, or any place. Ask permission to take a soil sample from the bed. Be sure to talk to your county Extension agent first. The agent can send you a special bag to put your soil sample in. Ask him or her how to take the soil sample, where to send it, and how much the test will cost. When the results of the soil test come back, show it to the garden's owners and tell them what they can do to improve their soil.

❀ Landfill Visit

Make a visit to a landfill. Many facilities have people there who can take your group on a tour and show you how your trash is disposed of. Be sure to let them know that you have been studying about composting.

❀ Wastewater Visit

Visit a wastewater treatment facility. Many facilities have people there who can take your group on a tour and show you how water is cleaned.

❀ Make a Difference

Create at least 12 large, colorful posters that tell people about composting. You may hang them on telephone poles, place them in store windows, or hang them at your school.

❀ Super Soil Business

Fill a few dozen large sealable plastic bags with compost from your compost bin. Sell the compost as a "super soil" to add to house or garden plants. Your group can sell the "super soil" for $1 for each bag at an open house at school, at a nearby business, or to neighbors. It is a good idea to put up signs to tell who is raising the money and how it will be used.

❀ Create Your Own

Your JMG group can have fun creating your own unique leadership/ community service project.

Circle the project you have completed.

_____date completed
_____leader/parent initials

Ecology and Environmental Horticulture

Balance and Interactions in Nature

Have you ever noticed that what you say or do affects other people? For example, if you throw away your soda can it may end up on the side of the road for someone else to pick up. Or, it may go to the landfill instead of being recycled.

In nature, there is a balance between all living things. Bees are a good example. Some people think bees just cause trouble, but many plants could not live without bees and other **pollinators.** Insects and animals that carry pollen from one flower to another are called pollinators. As bees crawl through flowers to get nectar for their hives they leave pollen from other flowers. When a flower is pollinated it can make fruit and seed. Because of this balance, the plants get what they need and the bees get what they need, too. When nature's balance is disturbed, problems occur.

Sometimes people do not realize that what they do affects this delicate balance between people, plants and animals. As Junior Master Gardeners, it is our responsibility to take care of the environment and this wonderful planet that is a home for all of us.

THINGS FOR YOUR JMG GROUP TO DO:

- ❋ Nature Class Web
- ❋ The Food Chain Gang
- ❋ Polluting Your Planet
- ❋ Exploding Cactus
- ❋ Garden Weather Station

THINGS FOR YOU TO DO:

- ❋ **Your Own World**

    Would you like to have your own world? You can make one! You can make a world with plants, living creatures, food for them to eat, and rain that falls down for all the living things to drink.

    Find a 2-liter bottle and cut off the spout. Fill the bottom of the bottle with soil and plant a small plant in the soil. Water the plant. Collect four or five insects such as crickets or pill bugs and drop them onto the soil. Pull a few leaves off a tree or shrub and crumble them onto the soil. Put your world in a spot that gets light but not direct sun.

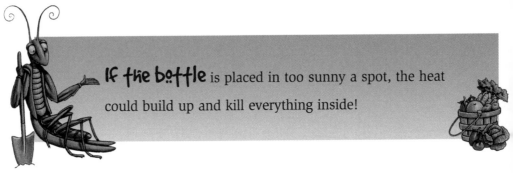

If the bottle is placed in too sunny a spot, the heat could build up and kill everything inside!

    Watch your world for the next few days. Look to see if the plants are growing, the creatures you caught are eating the leaves, and rain is running down the sides of the bottle.

_____date completed
_____leader/parent initials

❧ Wild Weeds

Sometimes gardeners work very hard to keep their plants healthy. Gardeners make sure that the plants they grow have the right kind of soil, the right amount of water, and the light they need. Some people even make sure their plants don't get too cold on frosty nights by covering the plants with cloth. So, why do weeds seem to be able to grow no matter where they are or what happens to them?

Weeds are especially tough plants with special parts that help them do very well even when they don't have good growing conditions.

Some weeds have very rough or hairy leaves. This helps them keep from losing their water.

Some weeds have very long roots that grow deep into the ground to search for water. These are called **taproots.**

Other weeds might have thorns on their leaves and stems. This helps keep animals from munching on them.

Search the area around your house or neighborhood and find:

Leaf with thorns
Draw a picture of what the leaf looks like.

Leaf that is hairy
Draw a picture of what the leaf looks like.

Taproot that is at least 8 inches long
Draw a picture of what the root looks like.

_____date completed
_____leader/parent initials

❊ A Bee's Eye View

Did you know that many insects and animals don't see the same way you do? Some animals don't see certain colors; some have eyes that see in totally different directions; and others have eyes that see even when it's very dark. Bees have special eyes, too. They can see colors on flowers that your eyes can't see.

Some flowers, like the one in the picture above, have special patterns in ultraviolet colors that help attract bees. You may know that plants need bees, bats and other creatures to help pollinate them so they can make seeds. Flowers that have these patterns have a better chance of attracting bees and getting pollinated.

In the petals of the flowers below, draw in a special design that you think would catch a bee's eye. Next time you notice a flower, remember that the prettiest part may be visible only to bees.

_____date completed
_____leader/parent initials

❀ Water Balance

If you make sure your yard is a place where helpful creatures can get water, you are also going to attract the pesky creatures. All living things need water. So how can you make sure to invite the helpful ones and not the harmful ones? Well, you can't. They'll probably both come! Remember, some of the pesky ones have to be there so the helpful ones can eat them!

Look for a place where water stands for a long time. It might be a pond near your home or a big container that is holding water. Check every now and then for a few days to see what creatures come to the water. Answer the questions below:

Where is the water? _____

How long has the water been there? _____

Did you see any birds come to take a drink? _____

What other creatures did you see come to the water? _____

_____

Is there anything living in the water? _____

Some insects such as mosquitoes will lay their eggs in standing water, but the water might also attract birds that will eat the mosquitoes. The helpful ones balance out the harmful ones!

_____date completed
_____leader/parent initials

❀ Become a Spider

There are many different kinds of spiders. Even though there are a few dangerous spiders, most are helpful because they eat many insects that can be harmful to your garden.

Some spiders chase after their food and others build traps and wait for their food to come to them. Orb web weavers are spiders that build webs in a circle pattern. Find string or yarn, tape and scissors. Then look at the steps to building an orb web below. Use the string to make your own web. You can make your web between the legs of a chair, in a doorway or on a Y-shaped stick.

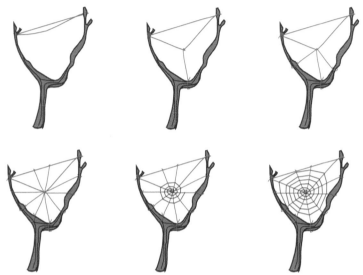

Once your web is finished, crouch down near a corner of your web just as a real spider might. Wait and watch for at least 5 minutes. Count how many insects you see in that time. You'll see spiders work hard to build their webs and patiently wait for long periods of time.

_____date completed
_____leader/parent initials

✿ **JMG Web**
Go to *http://juniormastergardener.tamu.edu.* Click on the Ecology and Environmental Horticulture button. Choose one of the activities under Balance and Interactions in Nature and complete it.

_____date completed
_____leader/parent initials

Habitats

When you invite someone to your house to visit it is nice to offer something to eat and drink. If you want wildlife such as birds, squirrels, butterflies, or other creatures to come and visit your home, then you should do the same thing. All living creatures need water and food, especially during the winter.

If you want wildlife to come and live around your home you must also provide **shelter,** which is a safe place for them to stay. This could be a nest, birdhouse, or plants and trees that the creatures like to live in or around. If you don't know what type of home creatures might like, then look out in nature. You can attract wildlife to your landscape by just copying what you see in nature.

THINGS FOR YOUR JMG GROUP TO DO:

- ❀ The Tree Community
- ❀ Gourd Bird House
- ❀ Our Pocket Park
- ❀ Backyard Buddy
- ❀ Visit with a Vet

THINGS FOR YOU TO DO:

❀ **Home Sweet Home**

You and all other living creatures need many things to be able to live. All living things need food to eat, water to drink, and shelter that can protect them. You have these things in your home. If you want to make your yard a home to helpful insects and other animals, you have to make sure that it offers food, water and shelter. Make your yard a home for these creatures and they will help you take care of pests and make your yard more beautiful.

Some creatures can find their own food and shelter if you give them water. Be creative. For example, if you can't buy a bird bath, you can use an upside down trash can lid, cake pan, or other container that's not too deep. Decide what kind of creature you want to come to your yard. Ask your JMG Leader what you need to make a home for it. Write down the name of the creature that you are trying to attract and what water, shelter and food is in your yard for it.

Type of creature: _____

What is the source of water? _____

What food is there for it? _____

Where can it find shelter? _____

_____date completed

_____leader/parent initials

❈ Toad Abode

Many people don't like frogs and toads, but they are goods friends to gardeners. Frogs and toads love to eat all kinds of insects. Many of the critters they like to eat are the same ones that eat the plants in your garden. You can invite frogs and toads to your yard by making a comfortable home for them to live in.

Find a clay pot. An old broken or cracked pot is best. Use a hammer to break off a section on the top edge of the pot. You should break off a piece about the size of a 50-cent piece. Put the pot upside down in a shady part of your yard. Soon a frog or toad may come to live and help keep the harmful insects out of your garden.

Search around your home for a pond or a ditch.
Look closely near the top of the water and you might be able to find tadpoles, which are baby frogs.

_____date completed
_____leader/parent initials

❈ Feathered Friend Feeder

Birds need food to eat. Most of the time they can find their own food, but sometimes they like to eat from a bird feeder. Bird feeders are easy to make. You will need a pine cone, peanut butter, birdseed and string. First, smear peanut butter all over the pine cone to make it sticky. Then pour the birdseed onto a paper plate or small dish and roll the pine cone around in it. Tie a string to the top of the pine cone and hang it from a tree. Now, watch the birds enjoy some great food.

_____date completed
_____leader/parent initials

✿ Boarding House

You can attract all sorts of creatures to your yard by giving them shelter. They don't need anything fancy and this activity will prove it. Lay a board on the ground and leave it for 1 or 2 weeks. When the 2 weeks have past, turn the board over. Count how many insects and other creatures you see. Draw pictures of the creatures on the board below. For help in identifying these insects, look at the pictures in Chapter 4.

_____date completed

_____leader/parent initials

✿ Journal

Pretend you are a bird that can write! In the lines below, tell what your perfect home would have in it. Describe how your home is comfortable for you as a feathered friend.

_____date completed

_____leader/parent initials

❋ **JMG Web**
Go to *http://juniormastergardener.tamu.edu.* Click on the Ecology and
Environmental Horticulture button. Choose one of the activities under
Habitats and complete it.

_____date completed
_____leader/parent initials

Hand-in-Hand with Nature

Everyone enjoys having a beautiful yard, school yard, or park to visit. We can
keep these green spaces looking great by removing things that could cause **stress**
for the plants and animals that live there. Many things can cause stress for plants.
Some of these are insect pests, diseases, not having enough water, or even too
much water. Would you like to work hand in hand with nature in your
neighborhood? Great! Here's how. . .just watch and wait. Often nature can take
care of itself without our help. For example, if a pest insect is feeding on a plant,
often a good insect will come and feed on the pest. To be hand-in-hand with
nature you must first look, see if there is a problem, decide if you need to help,
and be sure that if you do help it won't disrupt the balance of nature.

THINGS FOR YOUR JMG GROUP TO DO:

❋ On the Move
❋ Both Sides of the Fence
❋ Weighing Wastes
❋ Let's Try Organic
❋ Xeriscape

THINGS FOR YOU TO DO:

❋ **More Isn't Better**
Some people use chemicals to get rid of pests or fertilize their plants. These
chemicals can be a big help to gardeners if used correctly, but sometimes
people make a mistake and either don't use enough or, worse, they use too
much. When this happens they could be wasting their money and hurting
the environment. Usually they do this because they don't follow the
directions on the label. Just as it can be dangerous not to read directions
when you take medicines, it can be dangerous not to read the directions on
the labels of these chemicals. Pretend that you are going to use a fertilizer

on the plants in your garden. Look at the label and answer the questions below.

How much should you mix with a gallon of water?

_____

Can you just sprinkle the dry plant food onto the soil?

_____

How often should you use it?

_____

How much should you use if you are trying to sprout seeds? _____

Marvo Super Grow

10-20-10 Plant Food

Watch your plants grow to be super marvelous!

Wash hands thoroughly after application.

Directions for use:
Mix one teaspoon of Marvo Super Grow with one gallon of water. Mix well and pour onto soil. May be applied once a week. Do not apply until seeds have germinated.

If you use more than the label says, do you think the plant will grow even better? _____

Should you eat an apple while you are mixing up the Marvo-Super Grow?

_____

Show your answers to your JMG leader or another adult and always be sure to follow the directions on any label carefully.

_____date completed

_____leader/parent initials

❀ Organic JMG

Many people like **organic gardening.** This means they only use natural ways to take care of their plants and control the pests in their gardens. For example, organic gardeners might use compost from earthworms for fertilizer instead of chemical fertilizer. Or, they might release ladybugs in their gardens to eat up pesky aphids. You can try a safe and easy organic way to get rid of pests on your plants.

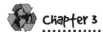

Look for a plant that has insects hurting it. Look to see if there are any helpful insects eating the harmful ones. If there are no helpful insects taking care of the problem, try spraying the pests with a water hose. This damages some insects or knocks them down to the ground where they can't hurt the plant. Go to the JMG web site for more organic gardening ideas.

_____date completed

_____leader/parent initials

✿ Water, Water, Everywhere

Water is a very important resource. You use water every day in many ways—drinking, bathing, and so on. Many times you use more water than you need to. Think about how you can use less water in all your activities. There are several ways to use less water, such as turning the water off while you brush your teeth and using water-saving shower heads. Write down ways you can conserve water.

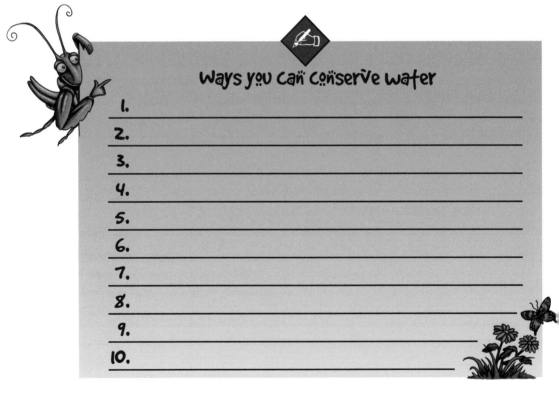

Ways you can conserve water

1. _____
2. _____
3. _____
4. _____
5. _____
6. _____
7. _____
8. _____
9. _____
10. _____

_____date completed

_____leader/parent initials

❀ Meter Reader

Water comes into your house every day. You can see how much water is used in your house by reading the water meter. Ask an adult to help you read the water meter at your house. You may have to really hunt for it! Circle an activity below that uses water. With the help of an adult, read your water meter before you do that activity and after the activity to see how much water is used. Also, read the meter at the start and end of one day, one week, and one month. This will tell you how much water is used in those time periods.

Activity (circle one)	Meter reading before	Meter reading after	How much was used?
Take a bath	_____	_____	_____
Wash dishes	_____	_____	_____
Water your yard	_____	_____	_____

	Meter reading at beginning	Meter reading at end	How much was used?
One day	_____	_____	_____
One week	_____	_____	_____
One month	_____	_____	_____

_____date completed
_____leader/parent initials

❀ JMG Web

Go to *http://juniormastergardener.tamu.edu*. Click on the Ecology and Environmental Horticulture button. Choose one of the activities under Hand-in-Hand With Nature and complete it.

_____date completed
_____leader/parent initials

Recycling

When you **recycle** you are actually turning trash into treasure. We can all make the earth a better place when we take the time to recycle. Did you know that plastic, glass, newspapers, and even tires can be recycled?

Nature has also been recycling for thousands of years. In the forest, leaves, twigs, and dead plants and animals are recycled to make rich new soil. How does this happen? Small microorganisms, fungus and even worms help break down these things to turn nature's trash into treasure.

Let's learn more about recycling!

THINGS FOR YOUR JMG GROUP TO DO:
- Vermi-composting
- Supermowing Machine
- Grow Cards
- Know & Show Recycling Sombrero

THINGS FOR YOU TO DO:
- **Grow Cards**

Have you ever planted a card that you got for your birthday or some holiday? In this activity you will make a card that you can give to someone, and they can plant it to grow flowers!

Look around your house and find scraps of paper. The paper can be computer paper, construction paper, or even newspaper. Tear up the paper into small pieces about the same size as stamps. Put the torn pieces in a blender until the blender is half full. Fill the blender with enough water to cover the torn paper. Blend until the paper mixture looks like mushy oatmeal. (Have an adult help you with the blender.)

Lay a cookie cutter on a screen that is over a sink or other container. Pour the paper mixture into the cutter. Allow the water to drain into the sink or container below. Sprinkle a few of your favorite flower seeds into the paper pulp in the cookie cutter and mash them down with your finger. Lift the screen off the container and place it on a towel. Remove the cookie cutter. Lay another towel on top of the paper shape and press to squeeze most of the water out. Let your paper shape dry for a couple of days. When it is dry you can attach it to a folded piece of brown paper bag to make a beautiful card.

Whoever gets the card can later plant it, keep it moist, and grow the gift that is hidden in the paper of the card.

_____date completed
_____leader/parent initials

❀ Use it...Don't lose it!

The next time you rake leaves in your yard or mow your grass, don't throw them away. Leaves and grass clippings make a great mulch to put around your plants in your flower bed or garden. Mulch is important because it helps keep the soil moist and helps prevent weeds from growing around your plants. Use some of your free landscape waste as mulch in your garden!

_____date completed
_____leader/parent initials

❀ Critter Condo

If your JMG group has a worm bin, you can make your own mini-garbage disposal that will make compost for your plants. Have an adult help you cut the spout off a 2-liter plastic bottle. Tear newspaper into strips and dip them into water. Fill the bottle half full with the wet paper strips. Drop a handful of worms onto the paper and cover them with a handful of soil. Wrap a piece of black construction paper around the outside of the bottle to keep the light out of the earthworms' new house. Place the bottle top into the critter condo with the spout pointing down. Now they're ready to work. Next time you have a banana peel or an apple core, bury it in the soil and the earthworms will turn it into compost! Then you can use the compost to make your garden soil better and feed your plants.

_____date completed
_____leader/parent initials

❀ Composting Homework

You may have already learned that you can make your own compost pile from grass clippings, leaves and other plant material. If you have a compost pile, you can also recycle newspaper, printer paper, and even notebook paper with old homework into compost. Keep a special wastebasket beside your trash can. Whenever you throw away recyclable paper, crumble it and tear it into small pieces about the size of business cards. Once that waste basket gets full, dump it onto your compost pile just as if it were a sack of leaves. Just think—the old homework papers that you compost today will help your plants grow better next year!

_____date completed

_____leader/parent initials

❀ Recycle Inventory

There are many things that can be recycled instead of thrown away. List below the things that your family is recycling.

1. _____

2. _____

3. _____

4. _____

5. _____

How can you tell if something can be recycled?

Look for the recycle triangle symbol

Are you throwing away some things that could be recycled? _____

_____date completed

_____leader/parent initials

❈ **JMG Web**

Go to *http://juniormastergardener.tamu.edu*. Click on the Ecology and Environmental Horticulture button. Choose one of the activities under Recycling and complete it.

_____date completed
_____leader/parent initials

Eco-Art

You can use things that you find in nature to make unique and special art projects and gifts. Many years ago people used things from nature to make dyes and paints, musical instruments, and even jewelry.

Let's have fun making Eco-Art!

THINGS FOR YOUR JMG GROUP TO DO:

❈ Plant Pounding
❈ Let's Dye It
❈ Nature Windows
❈ Garden Folk
❈ Nature Masks
❈ Mother Nature's Children

THINGS FOR YOU TO DO:

❈ **Seed Jewelry**

Start your own fashion trend by making jewelry from seeds you find. First, save seeds from foods you eat. They can be any kind of seeds you like—pumpkin, squash, watermelon, cantaloupes, or any other large seed. Or you can buy dried beans from the grocery store. Wash the seeds very well and let them dry completely. When you are ready to make your jewelry, soak your seeds in water until they are soft. Next, use a sewing needle and strong thread or unwaxed dental floss to string your seeds. Have an adult help you use the needle to pull the thread through the seed. You can make necklaces, bracelets, or anything else you can think of!

_____date completed
_____leader/parent initials

❀ Nature Garland

Go for a walk in your neighborhood or a park with a 5- or 6-foot piece of string. While you are walking around, collect some small objects such as twigs, grasses, flowers, nuts, bark and small rocks. Tie the first object close to the end of the string. As you walk along and find another interesting object, tie it on a few inches down the string. Keep walking until you have found several objects that catch your eye. When you get back home, look at each special object you collected and think about where you found it. Keep your Nature Garland and use it as a decoration in your room.

_____date completed
_____leader/parent initials

❀ Mystery Boxes

Tape the lid onto a shoe box and cut a hole in one end large enough to put your hand through. Decorate the box any way you like using crayons, markers, construction paper, or anything else you want. Cover the hole with paper and cut slits in it so that you can put your hand in it. Now put a mystery object inside the box. It might be shells, rocks, wood, leaves, twigs, nuts, or some other object from nature. Just make sure it will not hurt anybody. Let your friends put their hands through the hole and guess what is inside the box.

_____date completed
_____leader/parent initials

❀ Seeds Magnet

Cut a small shape out of cardboard or poster board. It could be a simple circle or square or a more complex shape such as a butterfly or leaf. Glue dry beans and seeds you've saved in patterns and designs that completely cover the cardboard. Attach a magnet to the back and use it as a natural refrigerator magnet.

_____date completed
_____leader/parent initials

❀ Recycle Sculpture

You can make art out of trash! Collect used cans, old boxes, cardboard tubes, milk jugs, and anything else you can find to create a sculpture. Try using tape or string to connect the objects. With an adult's help you might use a hot glue gun. Your sculpture can be any shape and any size. It is totally up to you because it is your recycled sculpture.

_____date completed

_____leader/parent initials

❋ Garden Folks

A fun way to personalize your garden is to create your own "garden folk" person. Attach a coat hanger to the top of a broomstick with tape. Put a plastic milk jug over the hanger portion of the coat hanger. This will be the head of your "garden folk" person. Use a permanent marker to draw a face on the plastic jug. Put the end of the broomstick in the ground so that your person can stand up. Now have fun dressing your unique "garden folk" person and make it come alive!

_____date completed
_____leader/parent initials

❋ JMG Web

Go to *http://juniormastergardener.tamu.edu*. Click on the Ecology and Environmental Horticulture button. Choose one of the activities under Eco-Art and complete it.

_____date completed
_____leader/parent initials

Leadership/Community Service Projects

Your group will choose one of the following activities to complete.

✿ **Winter Wildlife Tree**
In the cold months of winter, many animals are not able to find as much food as they do during the rest of the year. Your JMG group can create edible decorations for an outdoor tree that are beautiful and provide food for birds and other creatures.

✿ **Backyard Habitat Garden**
If you like butterflies, birds, squirrels, and other creatures in your garden, your group can invite even more of them by building a Backyard Habitat Garden. Certain creatures are attracted to certain plants. When your group plants them, you'll have these special creatures stopping to visit and building their homes in your own backyard, school or neighborhood!

✿ **Recycled Art Show**
Use the sculptures the JMGers in your group created to have an art show in your neigborhood. Your group could hold it at your school, a grocery store, a bank, or any other place in your area where people could see it. People might come by to vote on which recycled sculptures should be awarded prizes for the "Most Creative," or "Most Beautiful," or even "The Trashiest!"

✿ **Create Your Own**
Your JMG group can have fun creating your own unique leadership/community service project.

Circle the project you have completed.

_____ date completed
_____ leader/parent initials

Insects and Diseases

Insect Basics

Insects are around us all the time. If you piled up all the insects on earth, they would weigh more than all the people. (That's a lot of bugs!) Insects are everywhere, and play a very important role in the life of your garden. In this section, you will explore the world of insects by finding them, studying them, making them, and eating them!

THINGS FOR YOUR JMG GROUP TO DO:

- ❀ Insect Predictions and Survey
- ❀ Insect Symmetry
- ❀ The Great Cover-Up!
- ❀ Designer Bugs
- ❀ Insect Riddles
- ❀ Secret Smells Game

THINGS FOR YOU TO DO:

❊ Inspector Insect-a

Do you know that there are insects around us all the time? You may have to look closely, because many of them disguise themselves to blend in with their surroundings. Take a walk around your neighborhood and count how many different insects you see. Take along an empty jar with a hole punched in the lid so that you can collect a few insects. (Don't try to collect every insect you see—there are way too many!) After your walk, you can select a few insects to keep for your collection, or to use in making insect plaster casts, the next activity. Release the extra ones after you have finished observing them.

Make a list of the insects you saw, and the places where you saw them. According to your notes, where are the best places to find insects? What do you think makes these places especially "buggy"? Use the space below to record your observations.

Type of insect (or description)	**Where I found it**
_____	_____
_____	_____
_____	_____
_____	_____
_____	_____
_____	_____

Place where I found the most insects: _____

I think this place had the most insects because: _____

_____

Special note about collecting: Collecting insects can be a fun way to learn about them. To preserve them you can put them in a jar or plastic bag in the freezer overnight. If you prefer not to preserve insects, you can catch them to observe for a short time, and then release them.

JMG Trivia: The study of insects is called entomology. Ento means "insect" and ology means "the study of." A person who studies insects is called an entomologist.

_____ date completed
_____ leader/parent initials

❀ Insect Plaster Casts

Have you ever examined an insect up close? What did it look like? Insects are often difficult to examine very closely because they wiggle and squirm. It is easier to see what they look like by making an insect mold using plaster of Paris. You can also keep the mold for a long time, so that you can remind yourself later what the insect looked like.

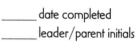

Find an insect that is either already dead, or freeze one for a day or two. Larger insects work best. Pour some wet plaster into a small paper cup to a depth of about 1 inch. You can make a mold of either the top side or the bottom side of the insect. Press the insect very slowly and carefully into the plaster, wiggling it slightly so that there are no air bubbles caught under it. Set the insect mold aside until it dries. When the plaster is dry, pry the insect out of the mold carefully. Use a toothpick or tweezers to get tiny pieces of legs and wings out of the mold. When finished, you will have a replica of your insect. You can also decorate your plaster cast with paint.

_____ date completed
_____ leader/parent initials

❋ Symmetry Snacks

If you draw an imaginary line down the middle of an insect's body, it will be exactly the same on both sides. Where there is a leg on one side of its body, there will be a leg in exactly the same place on the other side. People are the same way. If you draw a line down your body that divides you in half lengthwise, you will have the same features in the same place on both sides. Your body and an insect's body are **symmetrical.**

You can create a snack that is symmetrically decorated using two graham crackers, peanut butter, raisins, fruit bits, chocolate chips, or other small candies. Spread peanut butter smoothly over the surface of both graham crackers, and lay the two crackers next to each other. Pretend that the crackers are the wings of a butterfly, and decorate them in whatever pattern you like using the small food bits. Be sure the pattern is exactly the same on both crackers. Now you can eat your symmetrical butterfly snack.

Host an insect party by inviting a few friends over to create some symmetrical snacks.

_____ date completed
_____ leader/parent initials

❋ Camouflage Critters

When you go outside, there are insects all around you. However, you may not see them. To protect themselves from being caught and eaten, many insects disguise themselves so that they will blend in to their surroundings. This is called **camouflage.**

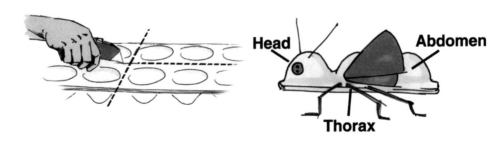

Head   **Abdomen**

Thorax

Make a camouflaged insect out of an egg carton like the one pictured on the right. Your insect has three body parts. It still needs six legs, a pair of antennae, and if you want you can add one or two pairs of wings. Use toothpicks, buttons or other items to add these parts. Decide what environment your insect will live in. For example, it might live on a tree trunk, on a blade of grass, in sand, or at another location. Paint your insect so that it is camouflaged to blend in to its environment.

_____ date completed

_____ leader/parent initials

❈ JMG Web

Go to *http://juniormastergardener.tamu.edu.* Click on the Insects and Plant Diseases button. Choose one of the activities under Insect Basics to complete.

_____ date completed

_____ leader/parent initials

Insect Life Cycles and Classification

Imagine being able to totally change your appearance. Instead of hands and feet, you might have suction cups for walking up walls. Or, you might grow wings and fly instead of walking. Imagine if you had different eyes that could see the world in dazzling colors. If you were an insect, these things could really happen! In this section, you will learn how insects transform themselves.

Because there are so many insects, scientists who study them have to sort them into groups. They sort them based on how they transform and what their bodies look like. Ready? Let's get going!

THINGS FOR YOUR JMG GROUP TO DO:
   ❈ All in the Family: Insect Flash Cards
   ❈ Ordering Insects
   ❈ Metamorphosis Bracelets and Belts
   ❈ Morpho Puppets
   ❈ JMG Web Activity: Journey North

THINGS FOR YOU TO DO:

❀ To be or not to be. . .an insect!

Look at the illustrations below and circle the ones that are insects.
Remember, an insect has three body parts, six legs, a pair of antennae, and
maybe one or two pairs of wings. Beware of sneaky imposters!

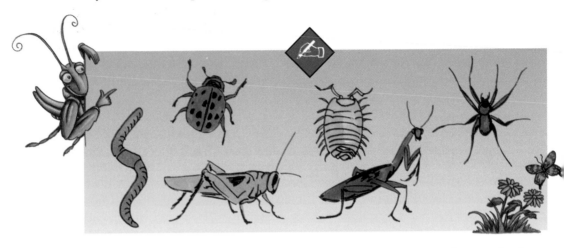

_____ date completed
_____ leader/parent initials

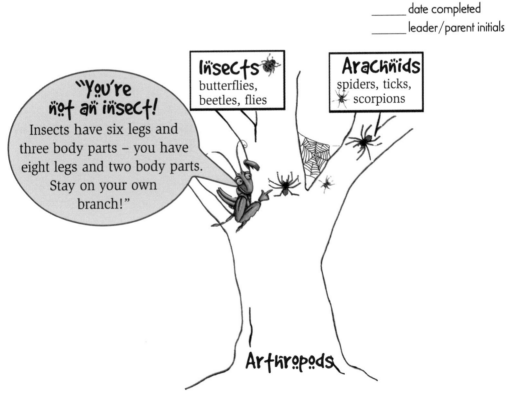

"You're not an insect!
Insects have six legs and
three body parts – you have
eight legs and two body parts.
Stay on your own
branch!"

Insects
butterflies,
beetles, flies

Arachnids
spiders, ticks,
scorpions

Arthropods

✤ My Family Tree

Find a photograph of your family and look at it. How are all of the people in it related? If it is your immediate family, there will probably be children and parents. Perhaps there are grandparents, aunts, uncles or cousins.

Fill in the blanks with the names of people in your family. Use the extra lines for the names of other special members of your family.

Do you know that insects have relatives and family trees, too? All living things, including plants and animals, are organized into family trees depending on how they are related to each other.

Be proud of your family tree. It is unique just like you!

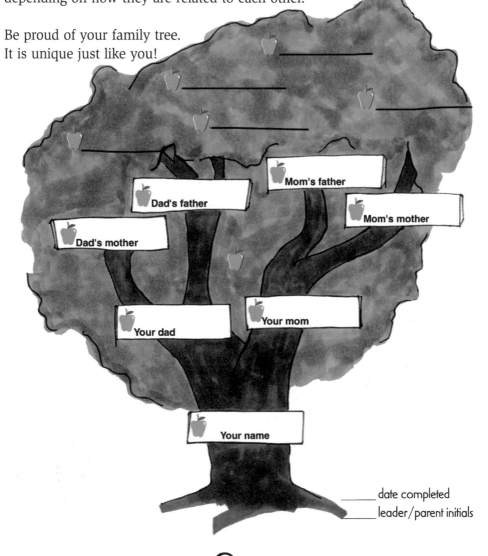

Mom's father

Dad's father

Mom's mother

Dad's mother

Your dad

Your mom

Your name

_____ date completed
_____ leader/parent initials

for your information: Look at the insects below. Each belongs to an insect group. There are many different groups of insects. The groups are called **orders.** Each order includes several families of insects that are alike in some ways.

Lepidoptera
butterflies and moths

- ✔ two pairs of wings
- ✔ complete metamorphosis (egg-larva-pupa-adult)
- ✔ chewing or siphoning mouthparts

Coleoptera
beetles

- ✔ two pairs of wings
- ✔ complete metamorphosis (egg-larva-pupa-adult)
- ✔ chewing mouthparts
- ✔ hard outer wings form a line down center of insect when closed

Orthoptera

grasshoppers, roaches and others

✔ two pairs of wings

✔ incomplete metamorphosis (egg-nymph-adult)

✔ chewing mouthparts

✔ large hind legs specialized for jumping

Hymenoptera

bees and wasps

✔ two pairs of wings

✔ complete metamorphosis (egg-larva-pupa-adult)

✔ chewing and sucking mouthparts

✔ narrow waists

✔ many live in social communities where they all work together

Diptera

flies

✔ one pair of wings

✔ complete metamorphosis (egg-larva-pupa-adult)

✔ chewing or piercing/ sucking mouthparts

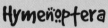
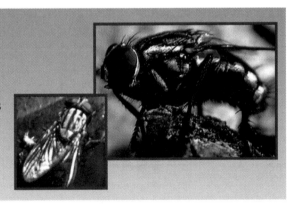

❀ Change as You Grow

Look at a baby picture of yourself. Have you changed? Probably so. However, you still have the same body parts as you did when you were a baby. You have two eyes, a nose, a mouth, two arms, and so on. When insects grow they go through a process called **metamorphosis,** which means "change of form." During metamorphosis insects change a lot. There are two kinds of metamorphosis. The most common kind is **complete metamorphosis.** Insects that go through incomplete metamorphosis do not change as much as those that go through complete metamorphosis. In **incomplete metamorphosis,** insects hatch looking like small versions of the adult insect.

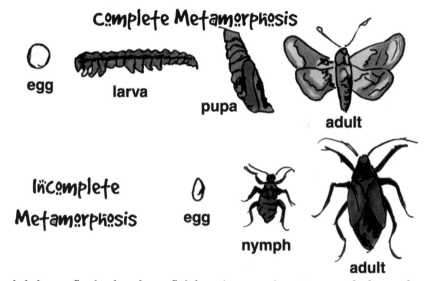

An adult butterfly (or beetle or fly) lays its **eggs** in a protected place where hatching **larvae** will be able to find food easily. When larvae hatch, they are eating machines! The more they eat, the more they grow. As they grow, they shed their skins several times. They do this because their skins cannot grow.

When a larva has reached full size it becomes a **pupa.** Sometimes a larva forms a cocoon to change into a pupa. Inside the cocoon, the pupa goes through many changes and becomes an adult. Soon the adult butterfly breaks out of the cocoon and the life cycle starts over again. Look at the picture on page 64 of this unit and see if you can find all four stages of the Swallowtail butterfly's life cycle pictured there. Show them to a friend or adult.

_____ date completed
_____ leader/parent initials

✿ Caterpillar Nursery

When butterflies are ready to lay their eggs they look for plants that will provide food and shelter for the larvae that hatch from their eggs. There are many plants that attract butterflies.

Go to a local nursery to find out about plants in your area that butterflies love. List three of them below:

_____

_____

Choose a plant that attracts butterflies and plant it at your home or school. It can be grown in the ground or in a container. Watch and see what butterflies come to visit.

Draw a picture in the box of the first butterfly that visits your plant.

Plants are food for the caterpillars (larvae). As the caterpillars eat and grow, the plants will look raggedy and bug-eaten, because they are bug eaten! You may want to plant your caterpillar nursery in an out-of-the-way area where the tattered plants won't show. Also, avoid spraying any chemicals in your nursery. You might accidentally kill your baby butterflies!

_____ date completed
_____ leader/parent initials

※ **Insect Island**

You will need:

✔ a caterpillar
✔ a large bowl
✔ water
✔ floral foam (available at florist shops or craft/hobby shops)
✔ branches of plant material for your caterpillar to feed on

Have an adult help you cut a piece of floral foam to fit inside your bowl. The floral foam should not touch the sides of the bowl because it is your island. Pour water in the bowl about 2 to 3 inches deep. Let the floral foam absorb water for about 15 minutes.

Where can you find a caterpillar for your island? You may be able to find one in a nearby field. When you find one, break off the branch of the plant on which it is feeding and stick the branch into your floral foam. Do not handle the caterpillar. As the caterpillar eats away the leaves, add more branches from the same plant.

Keep 2 to 3 inches of water in the bottom of the bowl to create an island for your caterpillar—like a moat around a castle. The caterpillar will stay on its island, feeding on the food that you provide. You can make an insect island for any insect that you want to observe, as long as you know what to feed it and it doesn't have wings.

_____ date completed
_____ leader/parent initials

❀ **JMG Web**

Go to *http://juniormastergardener.tamu.edu*. Click on the Insects and Diseases button. Choose one of the activities under Insect Life Cycles and Classification to complete.

_____ date completed

_____ leader/parent initials

Insect Collecting

Have you ever caught an insect? There are many places to look, and many ways to catch them. In this section, you can set a trap for insects, make an insect nightlight, and sweep up insects. Let's find out some ways to catch and collect them!

THINGS FOR YOUR JMG GROUP TO DO:

❀ Suck-A-Bug!

❀ It's a Small World

❀ Insect Nets

❀ By Land or Sea

❀ Ant Lion Farm

THINGS FOR YOU TO DO:

❀ **The Pitfalls of Being an Insect**

There are insects crawling everywhere. Some fly through the air, some live in trees and bushes, and many crawl around on the ground. You can catch insects that live on the ground using a pitfall trap. Use a glass jar or any small container for your trap. Find a spot that you want to investigate and dig a hole big enough for your container to fit in.

Place your container in the hole so that the top of the container is level with the ground. Pack soil around the container. Leave the lid off so that insects can get in. Next put some bait in the trap, such as a small piece of fruit or meat. Now you need to hide the trap by covering the opening with bark or leaves.

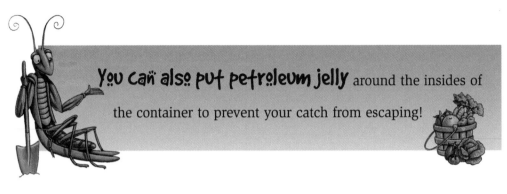

You can also put petroleum jelly around the insides of the container to prevent your catch from escaping!

Make two pitfall traps and place them in different areas of your yard or neighborhood. Check the traps every day to see what they attract. Did you find many of the same insects, or were they very different? Why do you think this is so?

_____

_____

_____

_____

_____

_____

_____ date completed
_____ leader/parent initials

❀ Let's Sweep Up!

There are many ways to catch insects, and a net is one of the best. You can make your own net very easily. Ask an adult to help you, and follow the steps on the next page.

You will need:
✔ a pillowcase
✔ coat hanger or heavy wire
✔ broom handle or dowel rod
✔ duct tape

1. Cut a hole in the outside layer of the casing on the side of the pillowcase with the seam.

2. Slide the wire into the hole and around the casing so that the pillowcase will stand open.

3. Leave about 4 inches of wire sticking out of the pillowcase on both sides. Attach the ends of the wire to the broomstick by laying the two ends of the wire along the broomstick and taping them down with duct tape.

Practice these two ways of using your insect net.

The Sneak Attack: Instead of chasing a flying insect, observe it closely. When it lands, sneak up behind it, holding the handle of your net in one hand and the tip of it in the other, and drop the net over the insect. This method works best with flying insects.

Sweeping: Hold the net in front of you, so the net is even with the top of the grass. Sweep the net from side to side, just as if you were sweeping your kitchen. At each end of a sweep, swing the end around so that the open end of the net comes first—like making a figure eight in front of you with the net. Once you get the hang of it, try walking and sweeping the net in front of you. After you make your last sweep, turn the handle so the net folds over the opening. This will keep insects from flying or crawling out of your net before you have a chance to check them out! Sweeping works great in yards and fields and can help you catch tiny insects that you don't usually see.

_____ date completed
_____ leader/parent initials

✿ Scavenger Hunt

Collect insects around your neighborhood using pitfall traps and your net. Make a list of the insects you find, where you found them, and how you caught them.

Insect	Where I found it	How I caught it
_____	_____	_____
_____	_____	_____
_____	_____	_____
_____	_____	_____
_____	_____	_____

_____ date completed
_____ leader/parent initials

❋ Insect Night Light

You will need:

✔ a white sheet
✔ something to hang the sheet over
   (a clothesline or tree branch will work)
✔ a black light that can be used outdoors
✔ an extension cord approved for outdoor use

A different group of insects is active at night, when you and the daytime insects are asleep. You can make an insect night light to trick the nighttime insects into hanging around after the sun comes up. Ask an adult to help you hang up the sheet, plug in the extension cord, and arrange the light so that it shines on the sheet. Leave the light shining on the sheet during the night.

Safety tip: If the light and extension cord are not intended for outdoor use, they are not safe to use and could start a fire. Have an adult help you with this activity!

Insects will be attracted to the bright light on the sheet. Many of the nighttime insects will remain on the sheet for a few hours the next morning. Check the sheet when you wake up to see what has appeared overnight. This is an easy way to observe nighttime insects that you don't usually get to see, without staying up all night yourself! Count how many insects you attract, and see how many you can identify.

Number of insects I found on my sheet: _____

Number of different insects I found on my sheet: _____

_____ date completed
_____ leader/parent initials

❀ Insect Collection

You will need:

✔ insects that have been frozen in the freezer overnight

✔ a pencil box or other box with a lid

✔ straight pins

✔ paper

Making an insect collection is a great way to preserve the insects that you catch. Follow the steps below to begin making your own personal collection of insects.

1. Stick a straight pin through the **thorax,** the middle body section, of the insect. Try not to put it exactly in the middle of the insect. Instead, stick it just to the right of the middle.

2. Make a label for your insect, with its name, where you found it, and the date. Stick the label on to the pin, below the insect.

3. Stick the pin with the insect and label into your box. Try to keep all the insects and labels at about the same height.

You can also wet a cotton ball with fingernail polish remover and place it in your collection jar to kill your insects. Ask your parents or another adult to help you with the fingernail polish remover, and check the label to make sure it contains ethyl acetate. It won't work without it.

_____ date completed
_____ leader/parent initials

❀ JMG Web

Go to *http://juniormastergardener.tamu.edu.* Click on the Insects and Diseases button. Choose one of the activities under Insect Collecting to complete.

_____ date completed
_____ leader/parent initials

Insect/Plant Interactions

Do you have a favorite color? Insects do, too. Many of the plants in your garden have flowers of a certain color just to attract a particular kind of insect. What do the plants want insects for? Read on and find out!

One thing plants need insects for is **pollination.** When insects pollinate plants then the plants are able to make seeds. Insects really can be a plant's best friend.

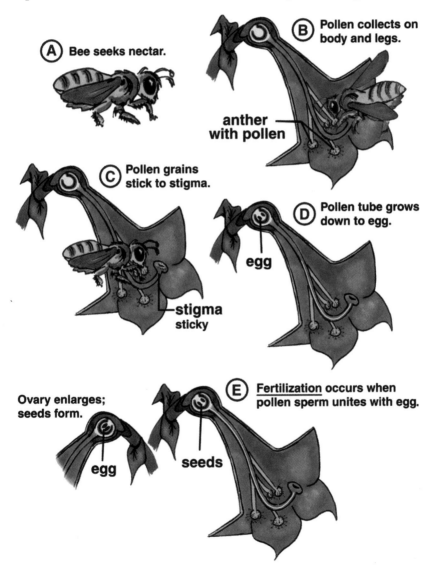

(A) Bee seeks nectar.

(B) Pollen collects on body and legs.

anther with pollen

(C) Pollen grains stick to stigma.

stigma sticky

(D) Pollen tube grows down to egg.

egg

(E) Fertilization occurs when pollen sperm unites with egg.

Ovary enlarges; seeds form.

egg

seeds

THINGS FOR YOUR JMG GROUP TO DO:
- Chew on This!
- Schoolyard Survey
- Pollinator Puppet Show
- The Bartering System
- The Lone Bee
- Designer Plants and Insects

THINGS FOR YOU TO DO:
- **Sign Language**

  In your garden you will probably see many insects. Most of them are friends of your garden, but some are garden enemies that will eat your plants. You may not be able to tell which they are just by looking at them, so it is important to know the signs of insect damage. When you walk across sand you leave behind tracks that are a sign you were there. Insects also leave signs that they have been on your plants. Look for signs of insect damage in your garden.

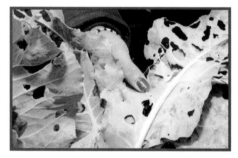 

Chewing damage is caused by insects with chewing mouthparts, such as caterpillars, grasshoppers and beetles. Chewing damage on leaves looks like bite marks you might leave on a sandwich.

Sucking damage is caused by insects such as aphids and spider mites that have straw-like mouth parts to suck out a plant's juices— sort of like using a straw to suck juice from a glass.

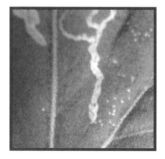

Tunneling damage is caused by insects called leafminers. An adult leafminer lays an egg between the leaf's layers. When the egg hatches, the larva tunnels through the leaf drinking the leaf's juice.

Honeydew is a sticky, gummy dropping that many insects leave behind when they feed on plants. It is made mostly of sugar, and attracts molds and fungus to the plant.

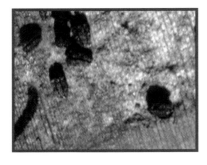

Frass is insect droppings (or bug poop!). Scientists can tell what type of insect caused plant damage by the type of frass left behind.

Hunt for signs of insect damage in your garden or around your neighborhood. Find an example of each of the types of damage pictured above.

_____ date completed
_____ leader/parent initials

❀ Good Gall-y!

Have you ever seen a strange-looking knot or ball on a leaf or twig? It's not a nut or fruit, or even a disease. It's called a gall, and it's actually plant tissue that grows that way because an insect laid its egg inside that part of the plant. When the insect hatches, it eats its way out of the gall and goes on its way. Galls are named for the way they look. Imagine what a hedgehog gall looks like, or a marble gall, or even a cherry gall!

Look around your neighborhood for galls. They can occur on many plants, but are very common on oak trees and hackberries. Many galls are caused by insects, but they can also be caused by bacteria, viruses and fungi.

_____ date completed
_____ leader/parent initials

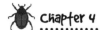

✿ Favorite Colors

What is your favorite color? Did you know that many insects and other animals have favorite colors, too? Many garden plants have flowers of a certain color to attract insects and other pollinators such as butterflies, moths, bees, wasps, and even beetles, flies and bats!

You can test insects' favorite colors by cutting flower shapes out of posterboard. Color each flower a different color. Attach the flowers to sticks using tape or glue and stake them outside. You can also lay them on the tops of bushes and plants. Place the different colored flowers a short distance apart so that you can tell what animals are coming to each color. Watch from inside to see what the flowers attract.

What did each color attract? _____

_____

_____

_____

_____

Remember, pollinators have to notice flowers while they are flying in order to be attracted to them! Try putting a group of flowers the same color together, and see if the group attracts more pollinators than a single flower.

_____ date completed
_____ leader/parent initials

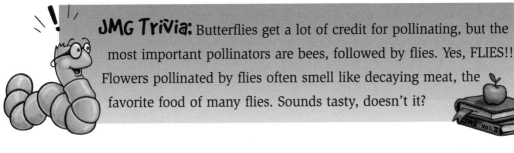

JMG Trivia: Butterflies get a lot of credit for pollinating, but the most important pollinators are bees, followed by flies. Yes, FLIES!! Flowers pollinated by flies often smell like decaying meat, the favorite food of many flies. Sounds tasty, doesn't it?

❋ JMG Web

Go to *http://juniormastergardener.tamu.edu*. Click on the Insects and Diseases button. Choose one of the activities under Insect/Plant Interactions to complete.

_____ date completed
_____ leader/parent initials

Insect Management

Before you squash that bug. . .WAIT! You might be squashing one of your garden's best friends. There are many more good insects than bad. Out of every 100 insects, only about two or three are harmful. In this section, you will learn how to tell your insect friends from your insect enemies, how to attract the helpful insects to your garden, and how to manage those pesky bad guys.

A pest is something that bothers you. In the garden, **pest** insects feed on your plants and disrupt their growth or harm them in a way that makes them less healthy. A **beneficial** insect is one that is helpful to you. There are four kinds of beneficials: predators, parasites, pollinators and poopers.

It is difficult to tell if an insect is a beneficial or a pest. Use the pictures on pages 88 and 89 to help you identify pest and beneficial insects in your garden. Remember, these are just a few common ones. Find a book at your library to help you identify others.

THINGS FOR YOUR JMG GROUP TO DO:
❋ Garden Friends and Foes
❋ Don't Bug Me!
❋ Who Goes There?
❋ Critter Creations

Beneficials

Predators prey on other insects. Ladybugs, praying mantids, dragonflies and spiders are all predators. Here are some predators you might find.

ladybug

praying mantid

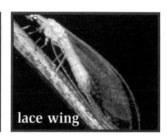
lace wing

Parasites destroy pest insects by laying their eggs on or inside of them. Here, a tomato hornworm carries tiny white eggs of Braconid wasps on its back. When they hatch, they will feed on the hornworm, eating it alive! There are many parasitic insects, but most are very small and go unnoticed.

Braconid wasp eggs on back of tomato hornworm

Pollinators are important to your garden because they pollinate many of your plants so that they can produce fruit. Here are some common pollinators.

butterfly

bee

wasp

Poopers, otherwise known as decomposers, provide nature's own recycling service in your garden. They eat, digest and excrete (poop) dead plant material. This allows the nutrients in the plant material to be returned to the soil.

earthworm

pill bug

dung beetle

For your information: Here are the top ten garden pests you might see in your garden.

corn earworm

aphids

tomato hornworm

spider mites

squash vine borer-larva

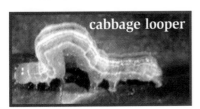
cabbage looper

cucumber beetle

squash vine borer-adult

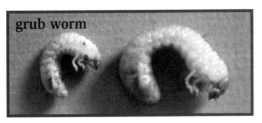
grub worm

mealybugs

THINGS FOR YOU TO DO:

❋ Attractor Factors

Beneficial insects will be attracted to your garden when pests are present, but you can also attract them and encourage them to linger by planting certain kinds of plants. Choose one of the ways to attract beneficials listed below and do it in your garden. Put a check by the method that you tried.

_____ **1.** Beneficial insects eat pollen and nectar when there are no pest insects to feed on. Many beneficial insects are very small, such as tiny wasps (nonstinging ones) and flies. Try growing plants with small flowers, such as alyssum or those in the mint (bee balm, basil, oregano), carrot (parsley, dill, Queen Anne's lace, yarrow) and sunflower (aster, zinnia, marigold) families. Choose two to plant in your garden.

_____ **2.** In your garden, include at least one flower, vegetable, herb and grass. Having a mixture of plants will reduce pests. Make sure that there are plants in bloom throughout the season. This means that beneficials will always have pollen and nectar to eat when there are no pests to snack on!

_____ **3.** Use a thick layer of mulch in your garden. Beneficial insects such as ground beetles and noninsect predators such as spiders use the mulch as a hiding place. Mulch helps cut down on weeds and conserves water in the soil, so it's good for the plants, too!

_____ **4.** Plant a patch of native wildflowers in or near your garden. This will attract native beneficials that will use them for shelter and food.

_____ date completed
_____ leader/parent initials

❋ Who Goes There?

Managing your garden is very important, and will make a big difference in how well your garden grows. Gardeners and professional horticulturists use a way of managing pests called **IPM,** which stands for Integrated Pest Management. IPM is environmentally friendly. Find three insects in your garden and follow the IPM steps on the next page for each insect.

My Insects

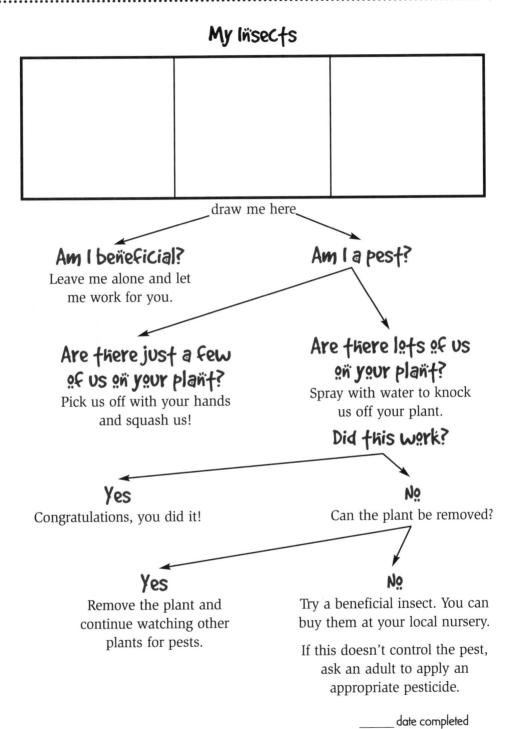

draw me here

Am I beneficial?
Leave me alone and let
me work for you.

Am I a pest?

**Are there just a few
of us on your plant?**
Pick us off with your hands
and squash us!

**Are there lots of us
on your plant?**
Spray with water to knock
us off your plant.

Did this work?

Yes
Congratulations, you did it!

No
Can the plant be removed?

Yes
Remove the plant and
continue watching other
plants for pests.

No
Try a beneficial insect. You can
buy them at your local nursery.

If this doesn't control the pest,
ask an adult to apply an
appropriate pesticide.

_____ date completed
_____ leader/parent initials

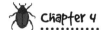

❀ Beneficials Abound

ladybug larva

Buy a package of ladybugs and release them into your garden. Many of them will probably fly away, but don't worry. Some of them will stay and munch on garden pests. To encourage more of them to stay, release them in the morning after you have sprayed the garden with water.

Make sure to release some of the ladybugs at the bottom of plants that have pests so they can find them easily. Ladybugs love to eat aphids and will lay eggs nearby. When they hatch, the larvae look like orange and black alligators, and they love aphids, too!

_____ date completed

_____ leader/parent initials

❀ Picture This

Use a sheet of paper, markers and other craft materials to create a garden scene. Include both beneficial and pest insects in your garden scene. It may be tempting to not show any pests. However, if there are no pests for beneficials to feed on, how long do you think the beneficials will stay around? Just like in your real garden, a balance of beneficials and pests is best.

_____ date completed

_____ leader/parent initials

Plant Diseases

Harmful insects are not the only bad thing that can happen to your plants. Plants can get diseases just like people. Fungi, bacteria and viruses are all around us and can make both people and plants sick. To help stay healthy you can eat nutritious foods, take your vitamins, exercise, and keep your body clean.

We can do things to help our plants stay healthy, too. By watering correctly, choosing plants that will do well in the garden, planting at the right time, and giving each plant its own space, we can do a lot to help plants avoid diseases. Keeping harmful insects away helps, too. Wow, you can do a lot to keep plants healthy and safe from disease. Prevention really is the best medicine.

THINGS FOR YOUR JMG GROUP TO DO:

- ❀ Exploratory Fungi
- ❀ Making Yeast Bread
- ❀ Lacy Leaves
- ❀ Like'n Those Lichens
- ❀ Prescription for Prevention
- ❀ There's a Fungus Among Us!

THINGS FOR YOU TO DO:

❀ **Fun with Fungi**

Have you ever seen a mushroom? What is it? It doesn't look like an animal, but it's not a plant either. **Mushrooms** are a type of fungus. There are many different fungi, and they are in an entire kingdom, all by themselves, separate from both plants and animals.

Most mushrooms grow in the forest where it is shady and moist. A mushroom has two parts. The part that you see is like the flower on a plant. It is the part that contains the **spores,** like seeds, that allow it to reproduce. The body of the fungus, sort of like the roots, stems, and leaves of plants, is buried in the layer of leaf litter on the ground. **Fungi** don't make their own food like plants do. They feed on dead leaves, twigs, insects, and other dead organisms.

Safety tip: Be careful with mushrooms that you find. Do not eat them or rub your mouth or eyes after handling them until you have washed your hands with soap. Not all mushrooms are safe to eat. Eat only mushrooms that you buy at the grocery store.

Find a mushroom growing in your garden or in some nearby woods. Dig around its base to see if you can see the root-like body of the fungus. You may be able to see some yellow or white threadlike strands around the bottom of the mushroom.

_____ date completed
_____ leader/parent initials

❀ Fungus in Your Food

What kinds of fungi do you like to eat? You may not know it, but you probably eat fungi every day, and like them! Fungi are used to prepare many foods. Look at the list of foods below. These foods are made with fungi. Circle the items that you like to see how many different fungi you eat!

cheese   pickles   bread

yogurt (plain and flavored)   sauerkraut   ice cream

sausage   soy sauce   mushrooms

What about foods with any of these ingredients, such as:

Pizza (bread and cheese)

Hamburgers (bread and pickles)

Sour cream (yogurt)

Any others? _____

_____ date completed
_____ leader/parent initials

❀ Mushroom Prints

Instead of seeds, mushrooms have spores. Spores are smaller than the tiniest seeds. In fact, 100,000 spores could fit in the period at the end of this sentence. Each type of mushroom has its spores arranged in a particular way. Scientists use these spore patterns to help them identify mushrooms. You can see these patterns yourself by making mushroom prints.

For this activity you will need two to three sheets of paper, a jar, and some fresh mushrooms from the grocery store.

Get a fresh, unopened mushroom like these.

Set the mushroom on a sheet of paper and cover it with a jar.

Leave the mushroom on the paper overnight, and check it the next day. When the mushroom ripens, the gill slits will open and release their spores. The spores make a pattern on the paper.

_____ date completed
_____ leader/parent initials

❀ Prescription for Prevention

In order for a plant disease to occur, there must be three things:

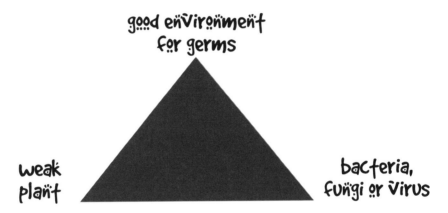

good environment
for germs

weak
plant

bacteria,
fungi or virus

If one of the three things is missing, your plants are protected from most diseases. The best way to prevent diseases is to keep plants healthy. Read the list of tips below and choose two techniques to practice in your garden. Make a check by the techniques you choose.

_____ **1.** Make sure your plants are healthy when you buy them, and use plants that are well suited for your area. (Your local nursery will be able to help you select good plants to use.)

_____ **2.** Check the tags that come with your plants or seeds. Space your plants just like the directions say. Overcrowded plants get thin and weak.

_____ **3.** Put a layer of mulch around your plants to prevent mud, which can carry fungi spores, from splashing up on your plants when you water.

_____ **4.** Fertilize your plants regularly so that they stay strong and healthy.

_____ **5.** Be careful when you water. Don't splash water on the leaves.

_____ **6.** Keep your garden clean! Don't let dead plants and weeds pile up because they can be home for many insect pests and plant diseases.

_____ date completed
_____ leader/parent initials

❀ There's a Fungus Among Us!

Fungi cause many plant diseases. Look at the pictures on this page. Try to find an example of fungi like these around your garden and neighborhood. Write down the name of the fungus disease, where you saw it, and what kind of plant it was on. Share your findings with family or friends.

black spot   powdery mildew   sooty mildew

_____ date completed
_____ leader/parent initials

❀ JMG Web

Go to _http://juniormastergardener.tamu.edu_. Click on the Insects and Diseases button. Choose one of the activities under Plant Diseases and complete it.

_____ date completed
_____ leader/parent initials

LEADERSHIP/COMMUNITY SERVICE PROJECTS

Your group will choose at least one of the following activities to complete.

❋ Collect and Share

Take a younger group on an Insect Expedition and show them techniques for catching and collecting insects.

❋ Butterfly Garden

If you like butterflies fluttering around your garden, your group can attract even more of them by building a butterfly garden. Certain butterflies are attracted to certain plants. Select some butterfly plants and plant your own butterfly garden in your neighborhood.

❋ Butterfly Release

Have you ever been to a ceremony and seen balloons being released? Why not try the same idea with butterflies? Your JMG group can raise your own butterflies to release at a school ceremony, garden dedication, or even at your JMG graduation! Check with your local nursery, county Extension agent, or the World Wide Web for resources.

❋ Create Your Own

Your JMG group can have fun creating your own unique leadership/community service project.

Circle the project you
have completed.

_____ date completed
_____ leader/parent initials

Landscape Horticulture

Design Process

A person who is a landscape designer looks at an area outside and finds ways to make it more beautiful and useful. If you had a spot that you wanted a landscape designer to improve, you would meet to talk about it. The designer would want to find out about you and your family, what plants you like, how you use your yard, and many other questions. He or she would also have to come look at your yard to find out things like: Is it a front or backyard? Does it get mostly sun or shade? Are there any plants in the yard that need to be removed? The designer wants to find out a lot about you and your area so the plan will be made just for you. This section will let you see what it would be like to be a designer.

THINGS FOR YOUR JMG GROUP TO DO:
- ❀ Rooms
- ❀ People and Places
- ❀ Money Trees
- ❀ Site Map

THINGS FOR YOU TO DO:
❀ Interview with a Client

People who create a design for where to put the grass, flower beds, bushes and trees in a yard are called **landscape designers.** When a designer makes a design for someone, that person is the **client.** It is important for the designer to find out about the client and what kinds of things the client likes. That way the design will be something that is made to fit the client. Ask someone to pretend to be your client. It can be someone in your family or a neighbor. Ask your client the following questions and fill in their answers.

Client Interview

Names of people in the family	Adult or child
_____	_____
_____	_____
_____	_____
_____	_____
_____	_____

If there are children in the family, the landscape would probably have a large, open area for playing.

1. Are there any plants that people in your home are allergic to? _____

You would be sure not to use these plants.

2. Are there any outdoor pets? Yes No

If there are pets or young children, you would not want to use plants that would be poisonous if eaten.

3. What do you do in your yard? (play, garden)

_____

4. What do you want to do in your yard? (vegetable garden, swim in your own pool) _____

5. Do you want a design for your front yard or backyard? (Circle one)

The whole neighborhood sees a front yard, so it is called a public area. The backyard is only seen by certain people, and is called a private area. Private areas are places that have more plants and quiet, personal spaces.

6. Do you want to work a lot or just a little bit? _____

Some landscapes will need a lot of work to keep them looking nice. If your client does not want to spend a lot of time working in the yard, you wouldn't choose beds that need to be weeded very often or flowers that need to be replanted every year.

7. Do you enjoy working in your yard? _____

8. Do you have any favorite plants? What are they?

_____

You would try to add these in the plan.

9. Do you want flowering plants? _____

Flowering plants are beautiful but it sometimes takes more time to keep them looking nice.

Add any other questions you think would help you better understand what your client wants.

_____ date completed
_____ leader/parent initials

❀ Check Out the Site

Another part of making a landscape design is seeing how the yard that you are working on looks right now. This is the **site survey.** It will help you decide how it needs to be changed. Look in your yard or a friend's yard and answer these questions.

Site Survey

1. Are there any spots on the site where water stands? Yes No

If so, most plants probably wouldn't grow well in that spot. Your plan might recommend filling in that spot with dirt or using special plants that like the wet soil.

2. Is the site sunny or shaded or both? _____

This would help you decide what kinds of plants to add to the site.

3. Where is the west part of your landscape? _____

The west and southwest parts of the landscape are the sunniest and hottest parts.

4. Is there grass on the site? Yes No

5. Are there trees and shrubs in the yard? Yes No

If yes, how many trees or shrubs are there and where are they?

_____

_____

_____

6. Are there beds at the site? Yes No

7. Are the plants that are already there healthy? Yes No

This would help you decide which plants should stay and which ones need to be taken out.

8. Does the site need more privacy? Yes No

If it does, your plan could add a fence or trees to help block the view from a neighbor's house.

9. Are there underground sprinklers in the yard? Yes No

Underground sprinklers save time in caring for the landscape, but they cost more money.

_____ date completed
_____ leader/parent initials

❀ Sun Watch

People who create landscapes have to pay close attention to the sun. Some plants like sun all day long and others only do well in mostly shade. Because the sun moves, some plants might get sun during part of the day and shade part of the day. Pick a plant or tree outside that gets some sun during the day and is healthy. Check the plant at each of the times below to see if it is getting sunlight or not.

For each time, circle the full sun if the whole plant is getting sunshine or the part sun if most of the plant is in the shade.

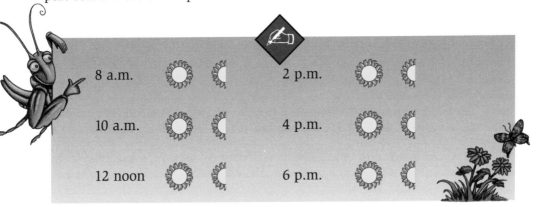

8 a.m.   2 p.m.

10 a.m.   4 p.m.

12 noon   6 p.m.

If a plant needs at least 6 hours of sunlight a day to be healthy, it is called a full sun plant. When you buy plants, most of them will have a tag that tells you how much sun that plant needs. If you plant it in the right spot, you'll help the plant do well.

_____ date completed

_____ leader/parent initials

⚘ Journal

Think about a place outside that you think is very pretty. Describe what it looks like on the lines below. Tell where it is, why you think it is beautiful, whether it has trees or other plants, how big the plants are, and what colors you see in this spot. Also think of one thing you could add to or change about this spot to make it more beautiful.

_____

_____

_____

_____

_____

_____

_____ date completed

_____ leader/parent initials

⚘ JMG Web

Go to *http://juniormastergardener.tamu.edu*. Click on the Landscape Horticulture button. Choose one of the activities under Design Process to complete.

_____ date completed

_____ leader/parent initials

Design Principles

Have you ever seen a vacant lot that is full of grass and weeds? Try to picture what that same area would look like if it was covered with green grass and big trees. Imagine that there were flower beds all along the edges, with many bushy shrubs and brightly colored blooms. You could even picture a small pond with a few orange fish swimming around the long, green leaves poking out of the water. Would you like to design an area to look like that? People who are landscape designers know tricks to making areas outside more beautiful. This section will help you learn the landscape designer's secrets.

THINGS FOR YOUR JMG GROUP TO DO:

- ❀ Nature Wheels
- ❀ Texture Collection
- ❀ Same Sides
- ❀ Does It Fit?

THINGS FOR YOU TO DO:

- ❀ **Potato Vase**

    If you have plants in a flower bed, they probably are not all the same size. The short plants should be in front of the tall plants so you can see them. Even if you are putting flowers in a vase, the tallest flowers should be in the back.

You can make a cool vase for flowers using a potato and straws. Cut a potato in half and set the flat side down on a plate. Poke several straws into the potato. The straws are going to hold your flowers! Decide which side of the potato will be the front. Use scissors to clip those straws shorter. Next, cut the straws on the middle just a little bit. Don't cut the straws on the back side. Fill the straws with water and find flowers that have stems small enough to fit in the straws. Make sure the plate for the potato has a little bit of water in it.

Look around your neighborhood and see if the beds in most yards have the taller plants in the back and the shorter plants in the front. Give your potato vase as a gift to a special person!

_____date completed
_____leader/parent initials

❀ Texture Rubs

The word **texture** means how things feel. Some things are very bumpy and others are very smooth. It is interesting when plants in a landscape have different textures. Plants get different textures from their leaves, flowers, and even their bark. Practice looking for different textures in plants and trees. Get some crayons and blank paper. Find trees and shrubs that have different textures in their bark and leaves. Hold the paper against the bark or leaf. Rub the long side of your crayon against the texture. Find at least five different textures of tree bark and leaves to rub.

_____date completed
_____leader/parent initials

❀ Color Wheel Complement

Has anyone ever told you that the clothes you were wearing didn't match? That means the colors didn't look good together. Colors in a landscape sometimes don't match either. It can be hard to tell which colors look good together.

Look at the color wheel. Colors on opposite sides of the wheel are **complementary** colors. That means they look good together. Find objects in your house or yard that are the same colors as on the wheel. You might find a blue marker, a red flower, a green blade of grass, and a yellow lemon. Lay the complementary colors beside each other and see if you think they match.

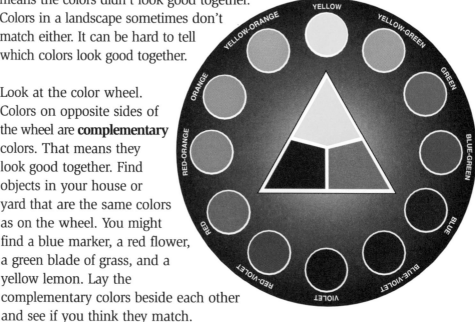

_____date completed
_____leader/parent initials

❄ Monochrome Mixture

Monochromatic means one color. Landscape designers sometimes use only one color in a space, but several varieties of it. For example, a design might use pale yellow, bright sunny yellow, and orange-yellow. This is called a monochromatic design.

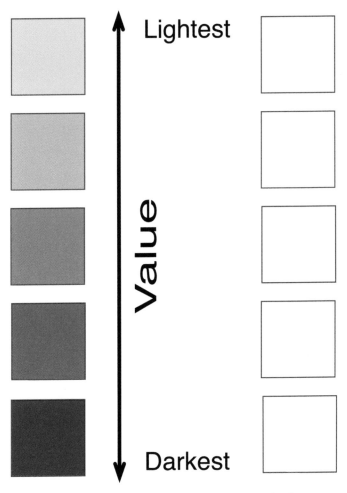

Look at the color wheel again. Choose one color and find a crayon in that color. In the boxes above, create your own monochromatic color pattern using the crayon. Mix this color with different amounts of white and black to make your color lighter and darker.

_____ date completed
_____ leader/parent initials

❀ Color Moods

Reds and yellows are called **warm colors** and they help to make us feel happy and full of energy. Landscape designers use reds and yellows to move people from one place to another. A good example of this would be putting a warm color near the front door to draw attention to your home. Blues and greens are called **cool colors.** They are used in spaces where people relax and spend time, such as backyards or other private spaces.

First, find two items in your house. One of them should be a warm color and the other should be a cool color. These could be two sheets of paper or anything that is easy to hold in your hand. Have someone stand 10 feet away from you with his or her back toward you. Ask the person to turn around and look at the items and then quickly turn back around.

Ask these questions:

What color did you see first? _____

How did that color make you feel? _____

_____

Name some familiar places where you see warm colors. _____

_____

Name some familiar places where you see cool colors. _____

_____

_____date completed
_____leader/parent initials

❀ JMG Web

Go to *http://juniormastergardener.tamu.edu*. Click on the Landscape Horticulture button. Choose one of the activities under Design Principles to complete.

_____date completed
_____leader/parent initials

Identification and Selection

You have already learned that some plants grow well in some places but not in others. For example, some oak trees wouldn't grow well in a place that is very cold and gets a lot of snow. Pansies wouldn't be able to live in a place that is very hot. Landscape designers have to make good decisions about what kinds of plants to put in certain spots. To be able to make those decisions, a landscape designer needs to know all about plants and what they need to be healthy. In this section you will find out about identifying plants and learn how plants are different.

THINGS FOR YOUR JMG GROUP TO DO:
- ❧ Tearing Trees
- ❧ How Tall is that Tree?
- ❧ Learning Your ABPs
- ❧ Great Green Grass

THINGS FOR YOU TO DO:
- ❧ **Is It Once or Always?**

    Go on a trip to a nursery or some other store that sells small plants. Read the tags that are on the plants. Did you know that some of the plants will last for many years but some plants will die after one season? If the tag says **"annual,"** that means it lasts for only one season. If it says **"perennial,"** it can last for many years. Do you want to spend money on plants that are going to last a short time or a long time?

    Many people use both types of plants because even though the annual plants live for only a short time, they have some of the prettiest flowers. List three annuals and perennials you found.

Annual

_____

_____

_____

Perennial

_____

_____

_____date completed

_____leader/parent initials

❀ Leaf Book

Collect leaves from as many different kinds of trees as you can. Whenever you find a leaf you like, put it between the pages of an old book or spiral notebook and leave it there for 2 weeks. Once it is dry, glue it to a blank sheet of paper. The pages can be saved in a folder or a binder. Label as many of the pages as you can with the names of the trees the leaves came from. Ask adults in your family or neighbors to help you identify the leaves. You can visit your county Extension agent, local nursery, or city forester for help identifying leaves. After you have several pages, show the book to your JMG leader and group.

_____date completed

_____leader/parent initials

❀ Superstars

One of the best rules for making a landscape plan is to plant what grows! While all plants grow, not all plants grow well in all places. To find out what grows well in your area, call someone who knows. Look in the yellow pages section of the phone book under "nurseries." Call one of the plant nurseries listed. Explain that you are a Junior Master Gardener student and that you need some information.

Say: I need to find out the best five trees and shrubs for growing in this area. Ask the person with whom you speak to spell the names of those trees and shrubs that you do not recognize. Be sure to say thank you when you are done.

Write the names of the five superstar trees and shrubs in the blanks below:

Superstar Trees	**Superstar Shrubs**
_____	_____
_____	_____
_____	_____
_____	_____
_____	_____

_____date completed

_____leader/parent initials

❀ My Tree Book

Select a tree in your yard to adopt for a year. You are going to make a scrapbook for the tree. Find two large sheets of construction paper, fold them in half, and staple close to the fold. This will be your book. On the front cover write the title "MY TREE BOOK" and your name. Each page will be for a different season—winter, summer, spring and fall. Write the name of the season at the top of each page.

Each page must have:

✔ A picture of the tree in that season (you can draw it or use a camera)

✔ A leaf from the tree (most trees are bare in the winter)

✔ A rubbing from the bark

✔ The date you made the picture

✔ Anything that might come from that tree (such as flowers or cones)

You'll see that some trees look very different each season and some stay the same all year long.

_____date completed

_____leader/parent initials

❀ Pine I.D.

Evergreens are trees that stay green all year long. Many evergreens have needles instead of leaves, and make cones. These trees are called conifers. Look for these trees in your neighborhood. There are three main kinds of conifers. Look at these pictures to see if you can tell the difference.

Firs

Short needles with blunt tips, leave round scars on branches

Pines
Needles grow in bunches, wrapped together at base

Spruces
Four-sided needles that are very sharp

Have somebody cover up the labels and see if you can remember the name of each of the conifers. Answer these questions:

Which conifer has long needles? _____

Which has very sharp needles? _____

How many sides do the needles on the spruce have? _____

Which conifer has short needles that are not sharp? _____

What are trees called that have needles and make cones? _____

_____ date completed
_____ leader/parent initials

❁ JMG Web
Go to *http://juniormastergardener.tamu.edu*. Click on the Landscape Horticulture button. Choose one of the activities under Identification and Selection to complete.

_____ date completed
_____ leader/parent initials

Installation

After you make a design and get the plants for a landscape, the next step is to plant them or **install** them. This section has activities to help you learn the best ways and times to install the plants in your landscape. If the plants are put in the ground correctly, they will be healthier and your landscape will be even more beautiful.

I. Till the soil of the bed you are planting.

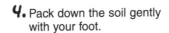

2. Dig a hole larger than the root ball you are planting.

(The root ball is the roots of your plant and the soil around the roots.)

3. Refill the sides of the hole with the soil you dug up.

4. Pack down the soil gently with your foot.

5. Water the soil around the plant.

THINGS FOR YOUR JMG GROUP TO DO:

❀ Arbor Day
❀ "Do It Right"
❀ Seed, Sod and Plugs

THINGS FOR YOU TO DO:

❀ **Make Your Bed**

Find a spot outside where you can make a flower or shrub bed of your own. Your bed should be only a few feet long. Before you can plant anything, you have to make your bed. To get the bed ready, first you need to break up the ground. This is called **tilling** the soil. Use a shovel to dig into the ground and turn the soil over. If the ground is too hard, try soaking it with water the day before you dig. Put compost or shredded pine bark on top of the soil about 6 inches high and mix it or "turn it" into the soil with your shovel. You can also mix leaves or grass clippings into the soil. This makes the soil better for plants to grow in. Once you've done this, your bed is made and it is ready for planting!

_____date completed
_____leader/parent initials

❀ Room to Grow

Some people make the mistake of planting trees, bushes and other plants too close together. When the plants are small they look nice close together, but when they get big, they get crowded.

Go to a nursery or other store that sells plants and trees. Find a small plant and a small tree that are for sale and look at the tags.

Write the name of the small plant:	Write the name of the tree:
_____	_____
How far away from another plant should this plant be placed?	How far away from other trees should this tree be placed?
_____	_____

Can you see examples in your neighborhood of plants that are too close together? _____

If you find some crowded plants, measure how close they are to one another? _____

How far apart do you think they should be? _____

_____date completed
_____leader/parent initials

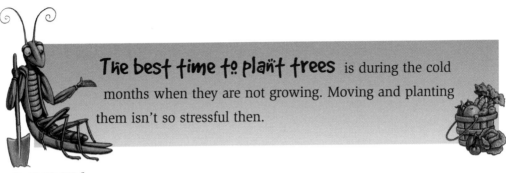

The best time to plant trees is during the cold months when they are not growing. Moving and planting them isn't so stressful then.

❀ **JMG Web**

Go to *http://juniormastergardener.tamu.edu*. Click on the Landscape Horticulture button. Choose one of the activities under Installation to complete.

_____date completed

_____leader/parent initials

Caring for Your Landscape

People spend a lot of time and money putting in a landscape. This is why it is important to take care of our trees and plants. Taking care of them will help them to grow and stay beautiful for a long time.

THINGS FOR YOUR JMG GROUP TO DO:

❀ An Inch Of Water
❀ Pruning Places
❀ More Mulch, More Moist
❀ Queen Bud

THINGS FOR YOU TO DO:

❀ **Dead Heads**

It seems that everyone likes flowers. Do you know the secret to making a plant have even more flowers? It is a trick called **dead heading.** Find a plant with flowers. Using a sharp pair of scissors, clip the wilted blooms that have begun to turn brown and die. Clip the stems right under the flowers. If a dying flower stays on a plant, the plant uses its energy to make the seed that is growing in the flower. When you cut off the old flower, the plant will use its energy to make more flowers.

_____date completed

_____leader/parent initials

❋ An Inch of Water

In this activity you'll learn how to water the yard properly so that you save money and keep from wasting water. When a sprinkler is on, water sprays out over a large area. If too much water gets on a yard, it will run off and be wasted. If the yard doesn't get enough water, the grass and plants could wilt.

When you water with a sprinkler, you want about 1 inch of water to fall into the yard. That is just the right amount to keep things well watered. How do you know when you have given the yard about an inch of water? You measure it!

Find empty coffee cans, mugs, or even cake pans. Put six of them in different places in your yard where the sprinkler water hits. Turn the sprinkler on for 30 minutes. Then use a ruler to measure how many inches of water are in each container.

Write down the amount in each container:

1. _____   4. _____

2. _____   5. _____

3. _____   6. _____

Leave the sprinkler on until some of the containers have 1 inch of water in them. How many minutes did it take? You may see that different containers get different amounts of water. When you water the yard, you may have to move the sprinkler around so all areas get an inch of water.

_____ date completed
_____ leader/parent initials

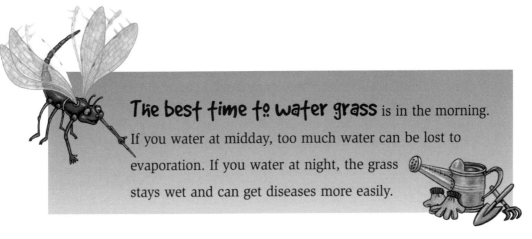

The best time to water grass is in the morning. If you water at midday, too much water can be lost to evaporation. If you water at night, the grass stays wet and can get diseases more easily.

❀ Clean Cut

Sometimes parts of a tree or shrub die. This can be for a number of reasons, including disease, drought, or freezing weather. The parts that die are called **deadwood.** It is important to cut deadwood off, so the plant can stay healthy.

When you have a cut or scrape, your skin heals. Plants can heal their cuts, too. When you cut the dead wood from a plant, the open cut area is a place where germs can get inside the plant and make it sick. To help the plant heal before germs get inside, you should make a clean cut. This means cutting in a straight line with a saw or special sharp scissors called **shears.**

Find two pieces of cardboard that are about the same size. Pretend the cardboard is a branch of a tree. Use something dull, like a butter knife, to cut one piece of cardboard in half. Use a marker to color the edges that were cut. This is the area where diseases can get into the plant. Now use some sharp scissors to cut the other piece of cardboard. Color the edges that were cut. Which cardboard has more colored area on the edge? That one is more likely to get sick. Show the cardboard to someone and explain why it is important to make a clean cut when getting rid of deadwood or pruning any branch.

_____date completed
_____leader/parent initials

🌸 Keep It Clean

The germs that make people sick sometimes spread from one person to another. That's why it's important to wash your hands before eating, and not share a glass or fork with someone who has a cold. The germs that make plants sick also can spread from one plant to another. This can happen if you use a tool such as a shovel, hoe or shears around a plant that is sick and then on another plant.

It is a good idea to clean your tools after you use them on any plant that might be sick. You can make your own germ-killing spray with an adult's help. Ask an adult to pour one capful of bleach into an empty spray bottle. Add nine capfuls of water. Spray the parts of the tool that touched the sick plant. Use paper towels to wipe the tool dry. Try not to get any of the germ-killing spray on you, and wash your hands after you use it.

_____date completed
_____leader/parent initials

🌸 Hey Bud! Let's Get Growing!

Look at the picture of the plant on the next page. The circles show special buds on the plant. These buds are the only places from which plants can grow. The red circle shows the terminal bud. This is the direction the plant is growing right now. The blue circles are the lateral buds. These are the places the plant could grow.

Sometimes a plant will grow long branches with few leaves. If you cut them off, the bottom part of the branch will grow bushier. Whenever the **terminal bud** is cut off, the plant sends a signal to the **lateral buds** to start growing. Use scissors to cut along the dotted lines on the picture. Then turn the page to see what the plant would look like 2 months later.

_____date completed
_____leader/parent initials

Before trimming

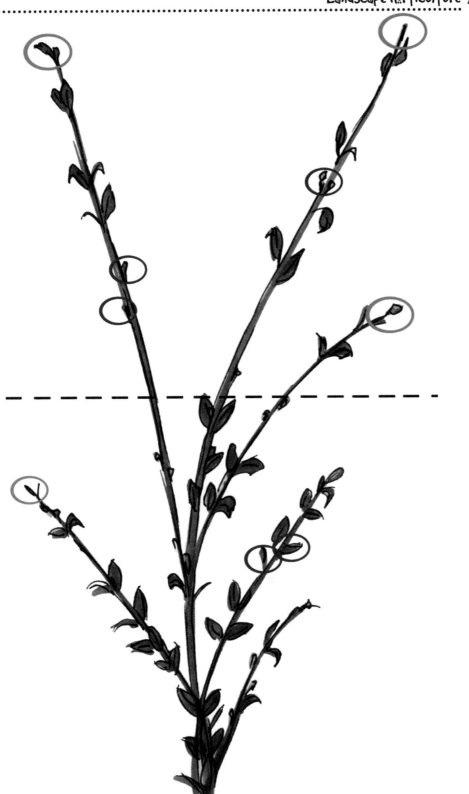

❀ Just Weed It

One of the hardest parts of keeping a landscape looking nice is removing the weeds that grow in beds. Getting weeds out of soil can be hard work, but it is easier if you have a small hand tool such as a trowel. Find someone in your neighborhood who needs help cleaning the weeds out of a flower bed. Pick a bed that does not have too many weeds, because that might require heavy work with a shovel before weeding. You might choose to help someone who would have trouble doing the job—maybe an older person or a mom with a new baby. Offer to weed the bed and politely refuse if the person offers to pay you.

Write the name of the person you helped here: _____

_____ date completed

_____ leader/parent initials

❀ Hole in One

Golf courses are very big and are covered with real grass. The special golf course grass grows close together and is mowed so it stays short. There is usually someone in charge to make sure the grass on the golf course stays looking nice. If you have a golf course in your town, have an adult call and ask if you can come and speak to the golf course superintendent. If you don't have a golf course nearby, you could visit the person who takes care of the grass on the Little League fields or school athletic fields. Ask the person with whom you visit about his or her job. Write the answers to the questions below.

What kind of grass do you grow here? on greens? on fairways? on fields?

_____

How often do you mow it? _____

How short does it have to be mowed? _____

How do you water the grass when it is dry? _____

Do you have to put any special chemicals on the grass? _____

Does the grass get damaged by insects or diseases? _____

_____ date completed

_____ leader/parent initials

Leadership/Community Service Projects

Your group will choose at least one of the following activities to complete.

❀ Plant a Bed

Almost any place will look more beautiful with flowers. Ask permission to plant a flower bed somewhere in your neighborhood or at your school. Good places would be around the flagpole at your school or in front of a nursing home. People at those places might even be willing to donate money for the project. Your group will need to:

1. get permission

2. interview the client and find out what he or she would like

3. conduct a site survey

2. prepare the soil

3. add organic matter

4. choose plants

5. make a design of how the bed will be planted

6. dig holes larger than the plants' root balls

7. put root balls in the ground and fill in with the soil you dug up

8. press down soil to fill in air spaces

9. water the plants

10. maintain the area or show the client how to do this

❀ Neighborhood or School Tree Book

There are probably dozens of different types of trees around your school and community. Your group could be the first to write a book to tell all about them. Each page could include a picture of the tree, a leaf, and information about the tree. You could include the scientific name, where the tree normally grows, how tall it gets, and any other information you find.

If you want to make more than one book, you can scan your pages with a computer scanner or have color copies made at a copy store. The group can design a cover and have it copied, too. The copy store could even bind the book for you. Then you could give copies of the book to local schools or city libraries.

❧ Annual Business
If your group wants to raise money, you could have an Annual Business. Annuals are plants that grow, bloom and die all in the same season. You can buy seeds and grow them to sell for your business. Your group will have to buy seeds, soil and containers. The amount you spend will determine the price you charge for the plants. The money your group raises can be donated to a charity or used to help your group do more projects.

❧ Wildflower Meadow
One very easy way to make a large area more beautiful is to spread wildflower seed. Your group will need to choose an area that will not be mowed regularly. Most wildflower seeds can be spread just by throwing them out and lightly tapping them into the soil with your foot. Be sure to give the seeds some water so they will start to grow. By spreading seeds, you can beautify a large area for years to come.

❧ Create Your Own
Your JMG group can have fun creating your own unique leadership/community service project.

Circle the project you have completed.

_____ date completed
_____ leader/parent initials

fruits and Nuts

Facts and History

You may have grown vegetables of your own, but growing fruits and nuts is not quite as easy. Most vegetable plants grow in one season and then die after they produce vegetables. Plants that die after one season are called **annuals.** Most fruits and nuts are **perennials.** That means they can live and grow year after year. Some fruit trees, such as apple trees, have to be a few years old before they can even make fruit. In this section you will learn about fruits and nuts, products of fruits and nuts, and how they grow. Do you want to plant trees like Johnny Appleseed, make your own peanut butter, and create designer apples? Keep reading and find out how!

THINGS FOR YOUR JMG GROUP TO DO:
- ❀ Dr. Fruit
- ❀ Linnaeus' World Wide Names
- ❀ Botanical Wood Prints
- ❀ A Bushel and a Peck
- ❀ Fruit and Veggie Lab

THINGS FOR YOU TO DO:

❀ Mr. Appleseed

John Chapman was born on September 26, 1774. He was famous for wandering through the country planting apple seeds. Many people believe he also gave the young trees, called **saplings,** to Indians and settlers. This earned him the nickname Johnny Appleseed. Some stories say that he wore a tin pot for a hat and a burlap sack for a shirt. We don't know how much of the legend of Johnny Appleseed is true, but we do know that John Chapman tried to make the world a better place.

Continue the work that Johnny started. Go eat an apple, and when you are finished remove the seeds. Put the seeds inside a damp paper towel in a sealed plastic bag. Put the bag in the refrigerator and check the seeds after 6 weeks to see if they have sprouted. Apple seeds have to think they have had a winter before they will sprout! If they have not sprouted, leave the seeds in the refrigerator for another 2 weeks. When they have sprouted, plant them about 1 inch deep in a small pot of soil. Make sure the pot has holes in the bottom for drainage. After the trees sprout and get a few inches high, give the saplings as gifts just like Johnny Appleseed did.

_____ date completed

_____ leader/parent initials

❀ Prized Peanuts

A famous scientist who was born in 1860 spent a lot of time studying about plants and how to grow them. He also invented many new and different ways to use plants. For example, he created more than 300 uses for peanuts and some people believe he even invented peanut butter. His name was George Washington Carver. He was famous for those discoveries but he was even more famous for the type of person he was. Although he had many inventions that could have made him very rich, he decided to give his inventions away. He said, "God gave them to me. How can I sell them to someone else?"

Junior Master Gardeners have something in common with George Washington Carver. Both help other people. Memorize the words of Carver and repeat them to an adult without looking!

"It is not the style of clothes one wears, neither the kind of automobile one drives, nor the amount of money one has in the bank that counts. These mean nothing. It is simply service that measures success."

Do something for someone today. Write what you did and who it was for in the spaces below.

_____

_____

_____

_____ date completed

_____ leader/parent initials

❀ Pomanders

Pomanders were worn by people about 500 years ago and were very popular. People wore them as decoration and for their wonderful smell. People weren't able to take baths as often as we do now, so pomanders helped people smell better! Back then, many people believed that pomanders helped to protect against disease. Today they are used as decorations and air fresheners in homes. They can last for more than a year. Make your own pomander with this recipe.

You will need:
- ✔ 1 orange, lemon, lime or apple
- ✔ 1 teaspoon allspice
- ✔ 1 ounce whole cloves
- ✔ 1/8 teaspoon ginger
- ✔ 1 tablespoon cinnamon
- ✔ 1 teaspoon nutmeg

Push the sharp ends of the cloves into the fruit with the big ends sticking out. Make sure the cloves in the fruit are close enough together to be almost touching. Continue until the fruit is completely covered.

Mix the cinnamon, nutmeg, allspice and ginger in a bowl. Roll the pomander in the bowl to cover the fruit with the spices. Shake the fruit and gently blow away the extra spice. Put the pomander in a brown paper bag and keep it in a dark cabinet for 2 to 3 weeks until it is dried and has shrunk. Then it can be given as a gift or kept to freshen your room.

_____ date completed

_____ leader/parent initials

❀ Global Fruit

At the grocery store you can find many different fruits all of the time. If fruits are ripe only during a certain time of year, why do we have fruits available year-round?

Go to your local grocery store and ask to speak to the produce manager. Find answers to the following questions.

Which five states in the United States produce the most fruits and nuts?

1. _____ 2. _____ 3. _____

4. _____ 5. _____

How long does it take fruit to get from the farm to the grocery store?

_____

What are your favorite three fruits in the grocery store?

1. _____ 2. _____ 3. _____

What country or state sent these fruits to your grocery store?

1. _____ 2. _____ 3. _____

_____ date completed

_____ leader/parent initials

❧ **JMG Web**

Go to *http://juniormastergardener.tamu.edu* and click on Fruits and Nuts. Choose one of the activities under Fact and Fiction to complete.

_____ date completed

_____ leader/parent initials

Products

Think about all the wonderful foods we get from fruits and nuts. What would the world be like without raisins or juice or peanut butter and jelly? Fruits and nuts give us many tasty, healthful snacks that we enjoy every day. In this section you will learn how to make some of these products and more!

THINGS FOR YOUR JMG GROUP TO DO:

❧ Snooty Fruit
❧ Apple-ing Appearance
❧ Taste Test
❧ JMG Jam
❧ Johnny's Appleslop

THINGS FOR YOU TO DO:

❧ **Jammin' Juice**

If you have a blender, you can make an incredible fruit drink. Pour 1 cup of your favorite juice in a blender. Next pour in 1 cup of water and a few ice cubes. Add half a banana, a few strawberries, half a peach, and a scoop of sherbet. Blend the mixture until it is smooth.

You can try blending any fruit or juice to make your own special flavor of Jammin' Juice!

_____ date completed

_____ leader/parent initials

❈ Grape Bake

Grapes are a juicy, healthful snack. You can make a totally different kind of snack by removing the water from the grapes. How can you do this? Bake them! When you bake them at a very low heat, they will dry out. You'll be surprised at how small they get once the water is taken out.

Rinse the grapes with cold water. Drop them in boiling water. After just a few seconds pour the grapes into a strainer to remove the water. Spread the grapes on a cookie sheet. Make sure they are not touching each other. Turn the oven on LOW or to 160 degrees. Leave grapes in the oven for 2 to 6 hours. Check them after 2 hours to see if they have finished drying out. Allow them to cool. What is another name for dried grapes?

Safety tip: You will need an adult to help with the Grape Bake.

_____ date completed
_____ leader/parent initials

❈ A Better Butter

Nuts are like meat because they contain a lot of protein. Nuts and meats even belong in the same food group. Can you think of a kind of butter that is made of nuts? Some people believe that peanut butter was invented by George Washington Carver. Some believe George A. Bayle, Jr. invented it. Others believe that peanuts were first ground up by Africans more than 500 years ago. Peanut butter is a healthful snack that can give your body protein to help build muscles. You can make your own peanut butter at home!

Put 2 cups of roasted peanuts in a blender. Add ¼ cup of sugar, 2 tablespoons of oil, and 1 teaspoon of salt. Have an adult help you turn on the blender and blend until the mixture is smooth. If you like crunchy peanut butter, add another ¼ cup of peanuts and blend a few seconds more. Enjoy your snack and thank the inventor of peanut butter!

_____ date completed
_____ leader/parent initials

❀ Journal

Taste two kinds of fruit you have never tasted before. Write down what those fruits are and tell whether you liked them or not in the lines below!

_____

_____

_____

_____

_____

_____

_____ date completed
_____ leader/parent initials

❀ JMG Web

Go to: *http://juniormastergardener.tamu.edu* and click on Fruits and Nuts. Choose one of the activities under Products to complete.

_____ date completed
_____ leader/parent initials

Growth, Development and Growing Techniques

Fruit starts out as a flower. When pollen from a flower touches the pistil of a flower, it could make new seeds. (See page 83.) When new seeds form, fruit grows around them to protect them. The seeds in that fruit could grow to make a new plant that can grow seeds of its own. People who want to grow their own fruits or nuts have to know the secrets of helping those plants grow. This section will teach you how fruits and nuts grow and what to do to help them grow better.

THINGS FOR YOUR JMG GROUP TO DO:
※ A Fruit's Life Rhyme (see Rhythms section)
※ Fruit Frenzy
※ The Zones
※ Just Chill
※ Fruit Factory

THINGS FOR YOU TO DO:
※ **Making Peanuts**

Did you know you can grow your own peanuts? Peanuts are just seeds, so to make your own peanut plant you have to find some uncooked peanuts and plant them. Put them between wet paper towels and cover the towels with a few sheets of wet newspaper. Keep the peanuts moist but not soaking wet. Soon the peanuts will sprout. When the roots are 5 inches long, carefully plant them in a sunny spot where the soil drains well, or in a pot with drainage holes.

As the plant grows, it will have flowers that will grow long **pegs** down to the soil. The part of the pegs that grows into the soil will make peanuts. You will know the peanuts are finished growing when the rest of the plant turns brown. Then it will be time to pull up the plant and remove the peanuts.

Once the peanuts are removed from the plant, it is time to roast them! Here's how to roast peanuts:

Place raw peanuts, in the shell or shelled, one layer deep in a shallow baking pan. Roast in the oven at 350 degrees for 15 to 19 minutes if peanuts are shelled and 20 to 24 minutes if peanuts are in the shell. Remove them from the oven and let them cool. Now you can eat and enjoy.

Or try microwave oven roasting
✔ 1 cup raw shelled peanuts
✔ cold water
✔ ½ tsp. salt

Pour the peanuts into a strainer and wet them thoroughly. Sprinkle them with salt. Pour them into a small microwave-safe casserole or pie plate. Microwave for 2 ½ minutes; stir and microwave 2 ½ minutes longer. Peanuts will be crisp when cool.

_____ date completed
_____ leader/parent initials

Safety tip: BE CAREFUL. Peanuts continue to cook as they cool. Cooking time may vary with ovens.

❀ Ripening Wrap
Some fruits tell each other when it is time to become ripe. Apples do this with a special chemical called **ethylene gas.** If you put a slice of apple in a plastic sack with a green banana, the gas from the apple will make the banana turn yellow quicker. Try it! Find two green bananas from the same bunch. Put one in a sack by itself and one in a sack with a cut up apple. Wait a day or two. Which one turned yellow more quickly?

_____ date completed
_____ leader/parent initials

🌸 Designer Apples

Red apples are not always red. Red apples don't turn red until the sun helps them to ripen. It is the sun that tells the apple skin to turn red! Have you ever seen an apple that is smiling? You can use the sun to make one.

Find a red apple that hasn't turned completely red yet. It might still be yellow on one side. Some apples that work well are Gala, McIntosh and Fuji apples. Cut out two circles for eyes and a curved smile from a piece of dark tape such as electrical tape or duct tape. Stick the smile and eyes to the yellow side of your apple and put the apple in a sunny spot or under a light. In 2 days, check the apple. You will probably see that the side facing the sun is now red. Remove the tape. The part of the apple that was covered by the tape is still yellow, leaving behind a smiling face in the skin of the apple.

_____ date completed
_____ leader/parent initials

🌸 Avocado Seed Soak

Have you ever grown trash? Avocados are one of the most healthful, nutritious fruits on the earth. When people eat them, they usually throw the seed away. Next time you get an avocado, keep the seed and let it dry out for a few days. Get three toothpicks and poke them into the sides of the seed. Fill a cup or jar up to the top with water and set the seed, with the pointed side up, on top of the jar.

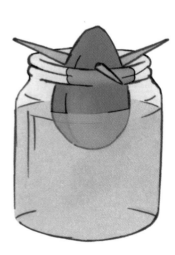

Check every few days and add water when the level drops below the avocado seed. After the seed sprouts and the roots grow about 3 to 4 inches long, plant the seed in a pot of good soil. Keep the plant in a sunny spot and keep the soil moist. Don't let it dry out and don't let it stay outside if it freezes. Soon you will have an avocado tree!

_____ date completed
_____ leader/parent initials

❀ Attractive Snacks

Birds and other animals sometimes eat berries. This is good for the animals, but it is also very good for the plants. How do you think that an animal eating up a plant's fruit could help it grow? Inside the fruit are seeds. When an animal eats the fruit, it swallows the seeds. Later the same seeds come back out of the animal when the animal leaves its droppings behind. When these droppings are left behind, a new plant may grow there!

Berries are usually bright colors so the animals can find them easily. When the berries attract birds and animals, they have a better chance of being eaten and dropped somewhere else to grow. Color the berries below in a way that would make them a very attractive snack for an animal passing by.

_____ date completed
_____ leader/parent initials

❀ Journal

Imagine you just discovered a fruit tree no one has ever seen before. On the lines below, tell where the tree is growing, what it looks like, and what the fruit looks like and tastes like. Also, think of a name for the new fruit you discovered.

_____

_____

_____

_____

_____

_____

_____

_____ date completed
_____ leader/parent initials

❀ JMG Web

Go to *http://juniormastergardener.tamu.edu* and click on Fruits and Nuts. Choose one of the activities under Growth, Development and Growing Techniques to complete.

_____ date completed
_____ leader/parent initials

LEADERSHIP/COMMUNITY SERVICE PROJECTS

Your group will choose at least one of the following activities to complete.

❋ **Share and Care Fruit Basket**
   Your JMG group can create a fruit basket featuring fruits and nuts from your state and deliver it to someone in need.

❋ **Create Your Own**
   Your JMG group can have fun creating your own unique leadership/community service project.

Circle the project you have completed.

_____date completed
_____leader/parent initials

Vegetables and Herbs

Planning the Garden

If you have ever worked in a garden, you probably know that the area didn't just become a garden by itself. It took a lot of planning and work. You have to pick the right spot and decide what to plant. You also have to decide where the plants will grow in your garden. The work you do with your JMG group and in this section of your handbook will help you plan ahead and make your garden a success!

THINGS FOR YOUR JMG GROUP TO DO:
- ❀ Home Sweet Home
- ❀ Make Your Pick
- ❀ Small and Large
- ❀ Rules are Rules
- ❀ Schedule It
- ❀ Some Like It Hot

THINGS FOR YOU TO DO:
❀ Garden Design

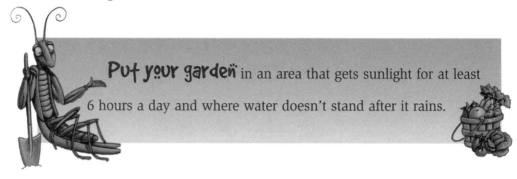

Put your garden in an area that gets sunlight for at least 6 hours a day and where water doesn't stand after it rains.

You have learned that vegetables must have enough space and sunlight to grow well. Follow the directions below to plant each vegetable in the garden outlined on the next page. Make sure your plants aren't too crowded. Fill the whole garden with radishes, squash and lettuce.

Radish

You will need to put 16 red dots in each square of your garden where you want to plant radishes. That's because about 16 radishes can grow in a square foot.

Squash

These plants need lots of room. Put one orange dot in the middle of four squares, because one squash plant can take up to 4 square feet in your garden.

Lettuce

You will need to put one green dot in each square where you want to plant lettuce. That's because one lettuce plant will take up about a square foot.

Garden outline

Each square represents 1 foot in your garden.

_____ date completed
_____ leader/parent initials

❀ Journal

Go to the grocery store or look in your own kitchen and write down ten vegetables or herbs that you find. Circle the ones you might like to grow in your garden. List them here.

_____

_____

_____

_____

_____

_____

_____ date completed

_____ leader/parent initials

❀ JMG Web

Go to *http://juniormastergardener.tamu.edu* and click on Vegetable and Herbs. Choose one of the activities under Planning the Garden and complete it.

_____ date completed

_____ leader/parent initials

Growing Techniques

Have your ever heard people say they have a green thumb? That means they are good at growing things. Their thumbs aren't really green, they just know what to do to keep their plants happy and healthy. Some of these things you have already learned in earlier sections of the Junior Master Gardener program. In this section you will learn more ways to make your thumb green!

THINGS FOR YOUR JMG GROUP TO DO:

- ❀ Cylinder Gardening
- ❀ Paper Towel Gardening
- ❀ Tender Transplants
- ❀ Weed Mats
- ❀ Season Extenders

THINGS FOR YOU TO DO:

❀ Creative Crazy Containers

Many plants grow as well in a pot as they do in the ground. For this activity, be creative and find a container that you don't normally see plants growing in. You might choose an empty soup can, a tissue box, or even an old tennis shoe!

Make sure there is some way for water to drain from the bottom of the container so the roots don't get soggy. Plant a seed in your container and keep the soil moist. If the container is big enough, let the plant grow. If not, transplant it into the garden once it has its second set of leaves.

_____ date completed

_____ leader/parent initials

❀ Zip and Grow

Find a sealable plastic bag and fill it with potting soil. Lay it flat on its side and cut one or two small Xs in the middle of one side. On the other side of the bag, make several small holes with a fork for drainage. Plant a seed that is in season right inside each X and water to make sure the soil is moist. Put it in a sunny spot and watch it grow!

_____ date completed

_____ leader/parent initials

❀ Radish Carpet

For this activity you will need help from an adult. Find a rectangular cake pan that is at least 12 inches long and 9 inches wide. Use a hammer and nail to punch several holes in the bottom of the pan so water can drain out. Go to a hardware store and buy a piece of ½-inch hardware cloth. Fill the cake pan almost to the

top with potting soil. Plant radish seeds about one inch apart and lay the hardware cloth over the top of the pan. Keep the soil moist and in about 4 weeks pull the screen up. You'll find a carpet of radishes. Wash the radishes and cut them up for a tasty salad!

_____ date completed

_____ leader/parent initials

❀ JMG Web

Go to: *http://juniormastergardener.tamu.edu* and click on Vegetables and Herbs. Choose one of the activities under Growing Techniques and complete it.

_____ date completed

_____ leader/parent initials

Harvesting

When a gardener or farmer works hard to grow the fresh vegetables and herbs that will end up in your kitchen, the work isn't over until the food is **harvested.** This means that the produce is taken from the plant so it can be eaten. How does a gardener know when it's time to harvest vegetables? How do you know which vegetables at the grocery store are fresh and ready to be eaten? The work you do with your JMG group and this handbook will help you learn how vegetables and herbs are harvested and how you can select the best ones at the grocery store.

THINGS FOR YOUR JMG GROUP TO DO:

❀ Garden to the Table

❀ Beauty Contest

❀ Seed Bank

THINGS FOR YOU TO DO:

❀ Seed Saving

Saving seeds is a way to collect seeds for free. The next time you eat veggies that have seeds, such as tomatoes, peppers and watermelons, keep some of the seeds. These seeds can be used to grow more of that same vegetable in your garden. Or, you can trade them with other JMGers.

_____ date completed

_____ leader/parent initials

❋ Watermelon Thump

Have you ever thumped a watermelon, squeezed a tomato or shaken a cantaloupe? Produce for sale at a market or grocery store may not be very good because it is not fresh or is not yet ripe. You already know not to buy vegetables that have bad spots on them. Also, don't buy anything that is soft or mushy. Try these tricks next time you go shopping so you can select the best produce.

Stick your thumbnail into a corn cob kernel. Choose corn that is juicy.

Hold a tomato and gently squeeze it. Buy tomatoes that are a little firm but not hard.

Choose peppers that are firm when you squeeze them.

Look for green lettuce that is not slimy or wilted.

Break a green bean in half. Buy them only if they are crisp and snap in two.

When you eat broccoli, you are eating flower buds that haven't opened. If you see any yellow flowers, the broccoli is old. Also, the broccoli should be crisp.

Shake a cantaloupe. You should buy the fruit if you hear the seeds inside rattle and it has a strong cantaloupe smell.

A good watermelon makes a "thud" sound when you thump it.

_____ date completed
_____ leader/parent initials

❀ **JMGWeb**

Go to *http://juniormastergardener.tamu.edu* and click on Plant Growth and Development. Choose one of the activities under Harvesting and complete it.

_____ date completed

_____ leader/parent initials

Nutrition in the Garden

"You are what you eat" is another saying you have probably heard before. It doesn't mean that if you eat a tomato you will become a tomato! It just means that if you eat healthful things your body will be healthy. In this section you will learn about the food you eat and ways to be healthy.

THINGS FOR YOUR JMG GROUP TO DO:

❀ The Pyramid
❀ Food Safety
❀ Label Reader
❀ Veggie Taste Test
❀ Junk Food Blues (see Rhythms sections)

THINGS FOR YOU TO DO:

❀ **Food Journal**

In the spaces below write down all of the food you ate yesterday.

	What did you eat?	How much did you eat?
Breakfast		
Lunch		

Snacks

Dinner

Circle the foods you think you should eat less of.

_____ date completed
_____ leader/parent initials

❧ Junk Food Blues Performance

Find "Junk Food Blues" in the Rhythms section of your handbook. Perform it for a family member, friend, JMG group, or school class.

_____ date completed
_____ leader/parent initials

❧ What Are You Eating?

You eat many different things in each day. Some of the things you eat are healthful and some are not as healthful. When you eat healthful foods, you are giving your body and mind a boost to be able to grow and work and learn even better. But, you have to hunt for healthful foods by reading the food nutrition labels. Food labels tell you the amounts of vitamins and other nutrients the food contains.

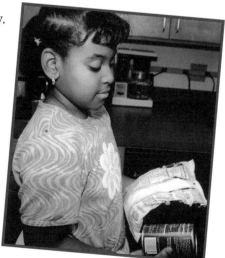

Look at the food nutrition labels on different foods in your kitchen cabinets.
Try to find labels that have at least one of the nutrients on the next page.

Vitamin A _____

Vitamin C _____

Iron _____

Calcium _____

Fiber _____

Hunt for foods that have the number 20% or greater beside one of the nutrients listed above. When you find a food that has at least 20% of that nutrient, write the name of the food in that blank. Fill in each blank and eat each of those foods sometime within the next few days!

_____ date completed
_____ leader/parent initials

❀ Making the Menu

This is a Food Pyramid. A Food Pyramid is a guide that shows you how much of each kind of food you should eat each day. Your job is to plan a menu for you and your family for an entire day. Try to plan your meals so your family eats the right amount and type of food.

During the day, you should make sure each person in your family eats:

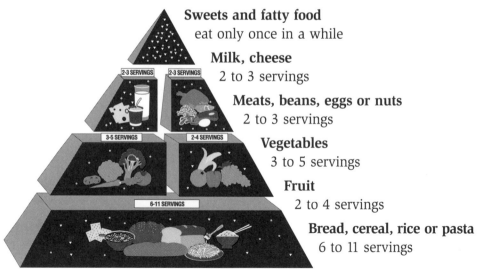

Sweets and fatty food
eat only once in a while

Milk, cheese
2 to 3 servings

Meats, beans, eggs or nuts
2 to 3 servings

Vegetables
3 to 5 servings

Fruit
2 to 4 servings

Bread, cereal, rice or pasta
6 to 11 servings

Write the menu you planned. Include drinks and snacks.

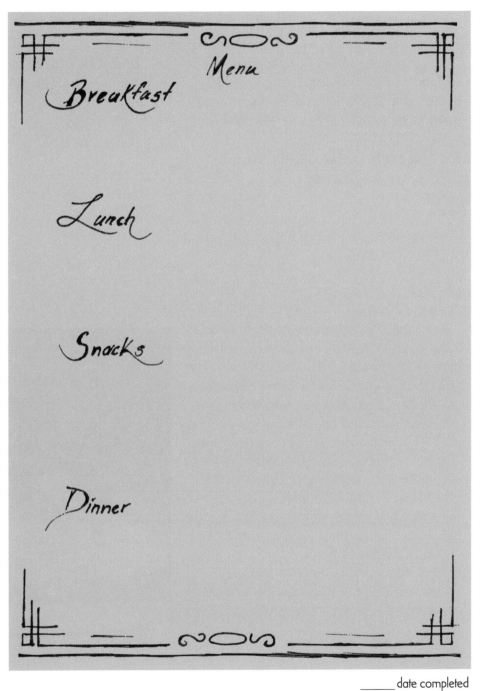

Menu

Breakfast

Lunch

Snacks

Dinner

_____ date completed
_____ leader/parent initials

Vegetable Products

Most people think that vegetables are just for food. Fresh, canned or frozen vegetables are probably a part of most of your meals, but veggies are also used for other things. Vegetables come from many different parts of the world. Vegetable products are used to keep people clean, make them prettier, make decorations for their homes, and make their soft drinks taste better. Veggies are even used in pepper sprays that police use to catch criminals.

THINGS FOR YOUR JMG GROUP TO DO:
- Garden Veggie Casserole
- Veggie Pizza
- Party Confetti Salad
- Cultural Cooking
- Garden Sponges

THINGS FOR YOU TO DO:
- **Vegetable Prints**

    Did you know you can create artwork with your food? When you cut a vegetable in half you see the shape of that vegetable and even a special design that shows how the insides developed. Find two or three different types of vegetables and have an adult cut them in half. Pat the flat side of the veggies with a paper towel and allow them to air dry for a few minutes. Use paint or markers to color the flat side and then press the flat side against white paper. If you have larger sheets of paper you can print your vegetable many times all over the paper to make wrapping paper. When decorating a large sheet of paper, you might want to use paints instead of markers.

_____ date completed

_____ leader/parent initials

❊ Interview with a Grocer

Think of three of your favorite vegetables or herbs. Write them in the blanks below. Go to a grocery store or market and ask to speak to the person in charge of produce. That person's job is to take care of all of the fresh vegetables, herbs and fruits in the store. Ask him or her the questions below to find out about the vegetables and herbs you eat.

Favorite Veggies: _____, _____, _____

Interview Questions

1. Do you have these three veggies in your store (your favorites)? _____

_____

2. Where were these grown? _____

_____

3. Do they grow in another place in a different season? _____

_____

4. How do you keep them fresh while they are in the store? _____

_____

_____

5. Write your own question to ask the grocer! _____

_____

_____?

_____ date completed
_____ leader/parent initials

❀ Veggie Critters

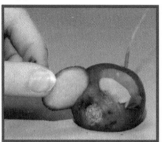

Vegetables can be used to create sculpture. Look at the pictures to get ideas for creating your own veggie critter. You may use only vegetables and herbs to create your critter. Have an adult help if you need to cut anything. Does it look like a person or animal, or is it just a special veggie critter? Tell what your critter looks like and what you used to make it in the spaces below.

_____

_____

_____

_____

_____

_____ date completed
_____ leader/parent initials

❀ Plant Detective

Did you know that there are lots of vegetables hiding in many of your favorite foods? Vegetables and other plant products are used in foods to make them taste good, and are also used in many other products to make them thicker and creamier. Look at the package labels for the items on the next page. Write down the plants that are in the ingredients lists.

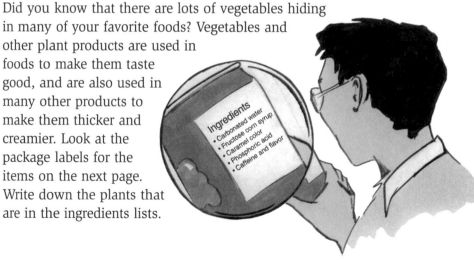

Ingredients
• Carbonated water
• Fructose corn syrup
• Caramel color
• Phosphoric acid
• Caffeine and flavor

Item	Plant Product
Soft drink	_____
Chips	_____
Candy bar	_____
Hand lotion	_____
Ice cream	_____
Salsa	_____
Instant drink mix	_____
Medicine/ointment	_____

Find five other items that have plant products in them.

l. _____

2. _____

3. _____

4. _____

5. _____

_____ date completed
_____ leader/parent initials

❀ Peanut Butter Celery

Vegetables make great snacks when you feel like eating something sweet.
Try this simple snack that is quick and healthful. Have an adult cut up
stalks of celery into chunks about 4 inches long. Wash the celery and spread
peanut butter in the inside of the celery. Make several of them and keep
them in a sealed plastic bag in the refrigerator for a few days. Whenever you
want a sweet snack, try peanut butter celery.

_____ date completed
_____ leader/parent initials

Herbal Products

For thousands of years, plants have been used for medicines, seasoning foods, and for their great smell. Different herbs are grown in different parts of the world. That's why foods from different countries have special flavors. For example, many Mexican foods include the herb cilantro, which has a unique flavor that makes pico de gallo, salsas, and even tacos taste so yummy.

THINGS FOR YOUR JMG GROUP TO DO:
- ❈ Touch and Smell
- ❈ Herbal Vinegar
- ❈ Herbal Bath Salts
- ❈ Herb Sachets

THINGS FOR YOU TO DO:
- ❈ **Ice Cube Seasonings**

If you grow herbs in your garden or buy them from a grocery store, they can be used for a long time to spice up your meals. Choose herbs you like and carefully rinse them. Have an adult help you chop up the herbs.

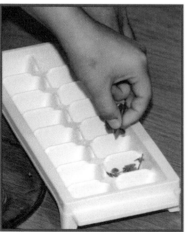

Find an ice cube tray and fill each section half full with chopped herbs. Carefully fill the tray with water and place it in the freezer. Once cubes are frozen, place them in a plastic bag and keep them in your freezer. Whenever a recipe calls for a teaspoon of an herb, try an ice cube seasoning instead!

_____ date completed
_____ leader/parent initials

✿ Rosemary BBQ Brush

If you have a rosemary plant and a barbecue grill, you can use the plant to brush barbecue sauce on the meats and vegetables that you grill. Clip five or six sprigs of the rosemary plant that are about 6 inches long. Rinse them carefully and tie their ends together tightly with string. Pour the sauce into a bowl and use the rosemary as a brush to paint your sauce on meat.

_____ date completed
_____ leader/parent initials

✿ Herbal Butter

Many people like butter as a topping for corn, potatoes or many other foods. It can be even better if it is flavored with fresh herbs. Put 6 tablespoons of butter in a bowl. Have an adult help you chop up any herb you like. Herbs that work well are parsley, chives, basil, oregano, dill and tarragon. Add 3 tablespoons of chopped herbs and a few shakes of salt and pepper to the butter. Use a spoon to mix and mash the ingredients together. Chill it in the refrigerator for at least 2 hours and share it with your family at dinner time.

_____ date completed
_____ leader/parent initials

✿ Mint Tea

To make mint tea, all you need is mint leaves, tea bags, water and a jar. Clip a handful of mint sprigs. Rinse them carefully and pull off the mint leaves. Put 2 or 3 inches of the leaves in the jar with one large tea bag or two small ones. Fill the jar with water. Cover the jar and let it sit in a warm, sunny place for 2 or 3 hours.

_____ date completed
_____ leader/parent initials

LEADERSHIP/COMMUNITY SERVICE PROJECTS

Your group will choose at least one of the following activities to complete.

❀ JMG Cookbook

In this chapter your JMG group learned about eating more healthful foods. Each JMGer should find one or two healthful recipes that use vegetables. Parents, grandparents and friends may have special recipes to share. Neatly write or type the recipes. Gather all of the group's recipe pages together and copy them. Also make a table of contents and an illustrated cover and copy them. Bind the book by stapling the pages. Cover the stapled edge with colored tape. Books could be given as gifts from the JMG group or sold as a fund raiser. You might give the money you earn to a local charity or use it to buy supplies for your group.

❀ Cafeteria Consultants

Is your school cafeteria serving healthful food? Does your school cafeteria manager want to know what the students' favorite and least favorite meals are? Make a list of several foods the cafeteria serves. Visit classes and ask students to vote for their favorite foods and least favorite foods. Create a graph to show these foods. Invite your school's cafeteria manager to visit your JMG group to tell you how he or she chooses what foods to serve. Show your graph to the cafeteria manager. If the school serves food that students like and eat, that means less food is thrown away and wasted!

❀ Veggie Fair

Many fairs across the country have competitions for home-grown vegetables. Your JMG group could do the same. Prizes are awarded for vegetables that are largest, best color, best shape, oddest, have the fewest blemishes, or any other award your group can think of. Your group could also hold a fair for recipes. Invite other students from your school or people from the community to be voters for your fair.

❀ Plant a Row

Many people in your community are hungry because they may not have enough money to buy the food they need. You can help them. Your group could contact a food bank in your area and find out what fresh foods they need. Plant a special section in your garden just for the food bank. As vegetables are harvested, clean them and take them to the food bank to help eliminate hunger in your community!

❀ Pyramid Presentation

You know there are some foods you should eat more of and some foods you should eat less of. The Food Guide Pyramid helps us to see how much of each kind of food we should eat. Your group can make a large Food Guide Pyramid poster using bright colors on poster board or bulletin board paper. Explain it to a group of younger children. You might lead an activity in which they cut out food pictures from magazines and decide where they belong on the pyramid.

❀ Harvest Fest

Plan and conduct a special harvest festival to celebrate harvest time in your group garden. Activities could include garden tours, taste tests, and scarecrow making.

❀ Create Your Own

Your JMG group can have fun creating your own unique leadership/community service project.

Circle the project you have completed.

_____ date completed
_____ leader/parent initials

Researcher

Floral Designer

Landscape Designer

Greenhouse Grower

Orchard Manager

Nursery Owner

Life Skills and Career Exploration

Self-Esteem

A wise old Greek man named Socrates used to walk around the streets of Athens saying, "Know thyself." He knew that if people did not understand themselves they probably would not be able to understand other people.

Understanding ourselves is not easy, because there are many things that make each of us unique and special. You are the only person exactly like you in the entire world! Some people have blue eyes, others have long legs, some have different colors of skin, and we all have different personalities. Some people are funny, others are shy, some people prefer to be with lots of people, while others like to be alone.

Exploring the differences in others is important. Let's start by learning more about ourselves.

THINGS FOR YOUR JMG GROUP TO DO:
❋ Who Are You?
❋ What Are You Like?
❋ Know Your JMG Friends

❀ Good JMGers Wanted Posters
❀ How Would You Feel?
❀ Feeling Bee

THINGS FOR YOU TO DO:

❀ **My Autobiography**

Learning about yourself can be fun. A story you write that describes you is called an **autobiography.** Fill out the questions below so that you can create your very own autobiography page.

MY AUTOBIOGRAPHY

My name is _____. I am _____ years old.

I was born on _____ in _____.

I have _____ brothers and _____ sisters.

My hobby is _____. My best friend is _____.

My favorite color is _____.

When I grow up I plan to _____.

Place a picture of yourself in this space or draw a picture of yourself.

_____ date completed
_____ leader/parent initials

❀ **Advertising Myself**

Have you ever seen a commercial on television for your favorite breakfast cereal? This is a type of **advertisement.** Advertisements (or ads) are used to try to persuade people to buy a product. Find five different advertisements for plant or food products. These could be can labels, magazine ads, or even ads from the newspaper. Cut these out and glue them on a sheet of paper. On another piece of paper use markers, pictures, or other materials to create an advertisement for yourself. You can use the advertisements that you collected as examples. This can be a way to show others more about you.

_____ date completed
_____ leader/parent initials

Relating to Others

It is not always easy to make friends, but it is fun when you do. To make and keep friends you must be a friendly person. Others will cooperate with you if you are friendly and helpful. Friends will be willing to share with you if you share with them.

Friends also help you learn how to get along with others. When you and your friends get together, you learn how to act in different situations. You learn to share, cooperate and take turns as you play together. Making friends and getting along with others takes time, practice and patience.

THINGS FOR YOUR JMG GROUP TO DO:
❀ Where's My Fruit?
❀ Let's Build It
❀ JMG Cooperation Roster
❀ Musical Chairs with a Twist
❀ Over and Under
❀ Cooperation Countdown

THINGS FOR YOU DO:

❀ Cooperation Collage

Collect old magazines, newspapers and pictures that show people cooperating with others. Some examples might be mothers taking care of babies, sports teams playing together, older children helping younger children, or even children on a playground. Glue these pictures to a poster board to make your own "Cooperation Collage." Hang this in your room as a reminder of why it is important to cooperate.

List below ways that you can cooperate with others in your JMG group.

_____

_____

_____

_____

_____ date completed
_____ leader/parent initials

❀ Let's Find Out

Make an appointment with a coach to discuss cooperation. This could be your school coach, soccer coach, baseball coach, or even a dance instructor. Ask them the following questions and write down their answers:

1. Why is it important to cooperate with others?	**2.** What happens if players on your team do not cooperate?

3. What is one example of how you help people on your team to cooperate? _____

_____

Be sure to thank the person for spending time with you and answering your questions. Share your findings with your JMG group.

_____ date completed
_____ leader/parent initials

Communication Skills

A long time ago, people communicated by drawing pictures on cave walls. Today, we communicate by writing letters, listening to others, talking to others, and even by computers through e-mail and the Internet. **Communication** is the process of sending and receiving messages. Sometimes we even communicate with others by our gestures and body language.

Every day we use communication at school, at home and at play. Learning to communicate with others is very important. To communicate with people, you must listen to their words as well as their body language.

THINGS FOR YOUR JMG GROUP TO DO:
- ❀ Garden Shed
- ❀ Who's On Our Team?
- ❀ Can You Follow Me?
- ❀ Plant A Seed

THINGS FOR YOU TO DO:
- ❀ **Cheer Cards**

  It is always nice to get cards in the mail. Think of someone who has helped you with your JMG project. That person would enjoy getting a card from you. You can either make your own card or get one from the store. Be sure to tell the person what you are doing in your JMG project and say thanks for the specific ways he or she has helped you. Before you put the card in the envelope, be sure to check your spelling. Put the correct address on the envelope and your return address goes in the upper left corner. Remember the stamp!

_____ date completed
_____ leader/parent initials

❋ Let Me Hear Your Body

Sometimes we can tell what people think and feel by watching their **body language.** Body language often tells more about us than the words we say. Listed below are three emotions. For each one, write down what your body does and make a drawing to show what happens to your body when you feel this way.

Happy
_____
_____
_____

Angry
_____
_____
_____

Embarrassed
_____
_____
_____

_____ date completed
_____ leader/parent initials

Decision Making/Goal Setting

Have you ever dreamed of becoming a movie star? Lots of people have dreams and are able to reach their dreams by setting goals. **Goals** are the steps we decide to take to reach our dreams. They are like a road map that helps us make good decisions. Goals can be short-term or long-term. An example of a **short-term goal**

is something you plan to do in the next few days, such as making your bed every day. A **long-term goal** is something you want to do over a long period of time. An example would be going to college, getting a job, or whatever your dream may be.

In order to reach a goal, you have to make many decisions. We begin and end each day with decisions. The choices that we make help us to adjust and reach our goals.

THINGS FOR YOUR JMG GROUP TO DO:
❀ Goal Search
❀ Right On Target
❀ The Class/Club Chronicle
❀ Watch Me Grow

THINGS FOR YOU TO DO:
❀ **What Are Your Plans?**

It is much easier to reach your goals if you write them down. Think about some of the things that you would like to be able to do in the next week. Write these down in the chart under short-term goals. Now, think about some things that you would like to be able to do next year. Write these down in the chart under long-term goals.

For each goal, you must think about how and when you will reach your goal. Write this next to each goal in the chart.

Copy the chart and put it in your room so that you can see it every day. Wait for 1 week and check your progress on your short-term goals. Share your goal sheet with a parent or friend.

Short-term Goals

What (you are going to do)	**How** (you are going to do it)	**When** (you are going to do it)
_____	_____	_____
_____	_____	_____
_____	_____	_____

Long-term Goals

What (you are going to do)	**How** (you are going to do it)	**When** (you are going to do it)
_____	_____	_____
_____	_____	_____

_____ date completed
_____ leader/parent initials

❀ Great Days

Every day we can find something good that happened to us. It is fun to keep a record of these happy times. In the space below, write down three good things that happened to you today. Share these with your family.

_____

_____

_____

_____ date completed
_____ leader/parent initials

❀ 4-H Record Book

One way to remember all the fun things that you did in your JMG project is to make a record book. A record book tells all about what you did in your project. It can even include pictures of you working on your project. Talk to your county Extension agent about entering the 4-H record book competition. County Extension Agents have all the forms and information you will need to do your very own record book. Now all you have to do is have fun completing your JMG 4-H record book.

_____ date completed
_____ leader/parent initials

Planning and Problem-Solving Skills

Every day we have to make plans and solve problems. It is important for all of us to be able to make our own decisions and solve our own problems. Some problems are easy to solve, while other problems are more difficult. In order to make a wise choice, you should get all the information you need, explore all your choices, and decide what action to take.

THINGS FOR YOUR JMG GROUP TO DO:

- ※ Making A Machine
- ※ Create A Costume
- ※ Pass It On
- ※ Either/Or
- ※ Let's Make a Case Out of It
- ※ It's In the Bag

THINGS FOR YOU TO DO:

※ Plan and Eat

One of the things we do every day that requires planning is preparing a meal. Pretend that you have $20 to prepare a meal for a family of four. The meal should be healthful, nutritious and delicious. It should include drinks, a main dish such as a meat dish, two vegetables, one fruit, and a bread. Decide what you would like to serve for your meal. You may need to look in magazines or recipe books for ideas.

	What I am serving	How much I need	Equipment I need	What it costs
Drink:	_____	_____	_____	_____
Main dish:	_____	_____	_____	_____
Vegetable:	_____	_____	_____	_____
Vegetable:	_____	_____	_____	_____
Fruit:	_____	_____	_____	_____
Bread:	_____	_____	_____	_____

Now that you've planned your meal, you must decide how much of each item will be needed for the four people in the family. For example, if you are serving corn on the cob, a serving would be one cob for each person. Check the food label on each item for the serving size.

Make a list of the equipment you need to prepare this meal. Ask an adult or friend to help you.

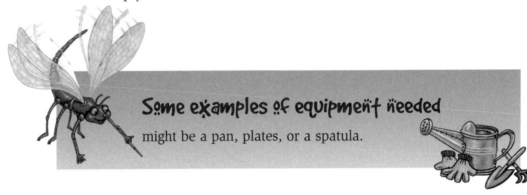

Some examples of equipment needed

might be a pan, plates, or a spatula.

By planning ahead and having your equipment ready, you will save time and do a better job of preparing the food. List the equipment you will need below:

_____

_____

There are several ways to figure the cost of your meal. You can go to the grocery store and check the prices, or you can read newspaper advertisements. It is important to see if there is a difference in cost between different brands. Is there a difference between fresh, frozen and canned food? If you are lucky enough to have a home garden, you can save money and use food from your garden in the meal. Add up the cost of each item on your menu. Is your total $20.00 or less?   Yes   No

If not, what could you do to make the meal cost less than $20.00?

_____

Share this menu with your family and help prepare it for a meal at your home.

_____ date completed

_____ leader/parent initials

❋ **Time Marches On**

There are 24 hours in a day. Have you ever thought about how you spend those 24 hours? Think about yesterday. What did you do? You had to sleep, go to school, eat, and do many other things. On the chart below, write down what you did for every hour.

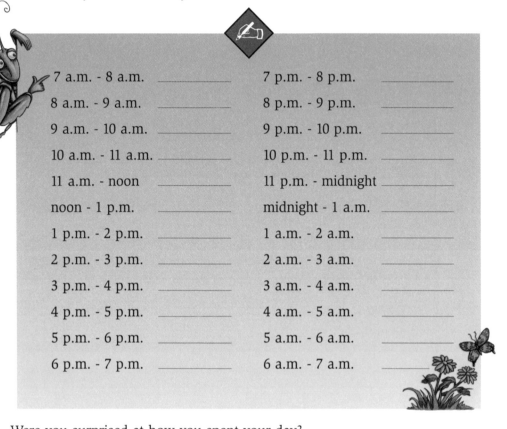

7 a.m. - 8 a.m. _____	7 p.m. - 8 p.m. _____
8 a.m. - 9 a.m. _____	8 p.m. - 9 p.m. _____
9 a.m. - 10 a.m. _____	9 p.m. - 10 p.m. _____
10 a.m. - 11 a.m. _____	10 p.m. - 11 p.m. _____
11 a.m. - noon _____	11 p.m. - midnight _____
noon - 1 p.m. _____	midnight - 1 a.m. _____
1 p.m. - 2 p.m. _____	1 a.m. - 2 a.m. _____
2 p.m. - 3 p.m. _____	2 a.m. - 3 a.m. _____
3 p.m. - 4 p.m. _____	3 a.m. - 4 a.m. _____
4 p.m. - 5 p.m. _____	4 a.m. - 5 a.m. _____
5 p.m. - 6 p.m. _____	5 a.m. - 6 a.m. _____
6 p.m. - 7 p.m. _____	6 a.m. - 7 a.m. _____

Were you surprised at how you spent your day? _____

List the three things that you spent most of your time doing.

1. _____

2. _____

3. _____

_____ date completed

_____ leader/parent initials

Responsible Behavior

What are some jobs that you are responsible for at your house? (Examples might be washing the dishes, folding clothes, raking leaves or feeding a pet.) Did you know that there are people in your school, JMG group, and family who depend on you to do your job? When everyone in a group does his or her job, things go smoothly.

Being responsible also means that you respect yourself and others.

THINGS FOR YOUR JMG GROUP TO DO:
※ Shared Responsibility
※ Consequences
※ Touchdown
※ Don't Stamp Me

THINGS FOR YOU TO DO:
※ **Who's Responsible**
In the first box below, write the names of all the people who live in your house. In the second box, list the different jobs that need to be done. Now, draw a line from the name of the family member to the job you think he/she would be good at. Family members can have more than one job. In some families one person does most of the jobs. Help your family find ways for everyone to help out!

My Home

My Family	Jobs to do

Look at the jobs you gave people in your family. Pick one or more for yourself and write the reason for your choices. _____

_____

_____ date completed
_____ leader/parent initials

❀ Proceed With Caution

When we are not responsible, accidents can happen. Your home or the place you play should be a safe place for you, your family and your friends. You can help by identifying things around you that could be dangerous. Let's take a look outside your home, school or community center.

Start in the front yard area. Find three potential safety problems. (Some examples might be toys in the driveway, tools left outside, water hose uncoiled, and others.) List them below:

1. _____

2. _____

3. _____

How could these be fixed? _____

_____

Who should be responsible for these jobs? _____

Go to your backyard. Find three potential safety problems. List them below:

1. _____

2. _____

3. _____

How could these be fixed? _____

_____

Who should be responsible for these jobs? _____

_____ date completed
_____ leader/parent initials

Career Awareness

The things that you learn in school help prepare you for a job that you can enjoy and that allows you to earn money to support you and your family. There are many jobs you might have some day. By learning about the many different types of jobs, you can decide what your future career might be.

THINGS FOR YOUR JMG GROUP TO DO:
- Careers and School
- Career Teams
- When I Grow Up
- Dream House
- All For One

THINGS FOR YOU TO DO:
How I Work Best
We all work in many different ways. Some people prefer to work in a group, others by themselves. Some people like to work inside, while others prefer to work outside. Knowing how you work best can help you decide what type of career you might enjoy. Let's find out how you work best!

I work best:

alone		with a group
inside		outside
daytime	or	nighttime
sitting down		moving
when it's quiet		when it's noisy

List three careers that fit the way you work best. Ask a parent or adult for help if you need ideas of different careers.

1. _____

2. _____

3. _____

_____ date completed
_____ leader/parent initials

❀ **Way Back When. . .**

Jobs of the past and the future are different. Many years ago, there were no computers. Today, computers are used at work, school and at home. Why, even the grocery store uses computers to check out your groceries and the library uses them to check out your books. Talk to a retired person about the job he or she had, and ask these questions:

1. What was your first job? _____

2. How much money did you make at your first job? _____

3. What job did you have the longest? _____

4. What did you like best about this job? _____

_____

5. What did you NOT like about this job? _____

_____

_____

6. How is this job different today than when you were working? _____

_____

_____

When you have finished your interview remember to thank the adult. Why not send a cheer card to show your JMG spirit!

_____ date completed
_____ leader/parent initials

❀ Career Book

One way to find out if a career is for you is to do some investigation. Put five sheets of paper together and staple them on the left side. This will be your career book. Pick a career that you would like to find out more about. Find information about that career to put in your career book. Find out what kind of education or training is required. Include pictures of a person working in that career. Write down the kinds of tasks you would do in that career. You could also interview someone who actually has that career.

Share your career book with your JMG group.

_____ date completed
_____ leader/parent initials

❀ JMG Web

Go to *http://juniormastergardener.tamu.edu* and click on Life Skills and Career Exploration. Select a career in horticulture and learn more about it.

_____ date completed
_____ leader/parent initials

LEADERSHIP/COMMUNITY SERVICE PROJECTS

Your group will choose at least one of the following activities to complete.

❀ **Career Display**

Contact your school or local librarian and ask if you can make a display about the career opportunities that your JMG group studied.

❀ **Job Shadow**

Contact a person working in a career that your JMG group would like to learn more about. Make an appointment to go and visit this person on the job.

❀ **Learning to Share**

Teach one of the life skill/career activities that your JMG group did to a group of younger children.

❀ **Create Your Own**

Your JMG group can have fun creating your own unique leadership/ community service project.

Circle the project you have completed.

_____ date completed
_____ leader/parent initials

Choo-Choo Song

From Chapter 1, Plant Growth and Development, page 4

Tomato sat on the railroad track,
Thought he was the boss,
Along came the choo-choo train, (clap)
Tomato sauce.

Avocado sat on the railroad track,
All jolly and rolly,
Along came the choo-choo train, (clap)
Guacamole.

Cucumber sat on the railroad track,
For this there is no excuse,
Along came the choo-choo train, (clap)
Pickle juice.

Other Verses

Blueberry, huffin and puffin, (clap) Blueberry muffin
Apple, playing with a spider, (clap) Apple cider
Lemon, where he often stayed, (clap) Lemonade
Strawberry, being such a ham, (clap) Strawberry jam
Orange, silly as a goose, (clap) Orange juice
Grape, Sunning his fat belly, (clap) Grape jelly
Onion, Doing his own thing, (clap) Onion ring
Potato, Wishing he could fly, (clap) French fry

Plant Parts Rap

From Chapter 1, Plant Growth and Development, page 8

Plants are our friends, we give them special care.
They feed, they shelter, they give us fresh air.

Without plants in our world, we simply could not live,
because of all of the awesome gifts that they give.

The tiny plant begins as a seed that germinates.
And from this moment on, here's the journey that it takes:

The roots are in the dirt to help the plant grow
and hold it in place when the winds blow.

Just like a soda straw, they suck up H_2O.
And when the plant gets water, stand back and watch it grow.

Stems hold the plant up, they carry water to
the leaves, flowers, fruit and seeds—that's what the stems do.

Leaves grow from the stem. They soak up lots of sun.
When they change it into food, then their job is done.

The food is for the plant—it gives it strength and power.
It helps it to grow and make a nice flower.

Wind, birds, and bees—these are a flower's friend.
They help the life cycle to start once again.

The flower makes a fruit with a seed deep inside.
Some are eaten, some are blown, or some just hitch a ride.

Once a fruit is dried and a little seed comes out,
the seed will find the dirt and a new plant will sprout.

Coconut Float

From Chapter 1, Plant Growth and Development, page 12

Once a young seed said to its big Mother plant,
"I want to stay with you!" She said, "I'm sorry seed—you can't."

"You need your own piece of earth—a place where you can grow."
Then the trees began to rustle and strong winds began to blow.

The seed was pulled far away and carried by the winds.
It fell lonely to the ground, but soon it made some friends.

A squirrel scampered by with some seeds in his cheeks.
It buried seeds all over, to hide them for a week.

The squirrel forgot about them and they began to sprout.
Those plants were growing strong when they heard a bird call out.

That bird squawked, "Watch out!"—earlier he'd been eating berries.
And now the bird was dropping droppings his body could no longer carry.

The droppings landed with a "SPLAT" in the open field.
From the seeds in that pile sprouted a plant that grows there still.

Soon a cat trotted by with stickers in its tail.
It stopped and scratched to get them out and on the ground they fell.

Those stickers were seeds that sprouted, now a huge bush grows there.
So if you walk in that area, be sure to take great care.

Another young plant that came nearby traveled far and at slow speed.
A coconut tree dropped a nut on the beach. Yes—a coconut is a seed.

The coconut did not grow on that beach, it got washed out to the ocean.
It traveled across great distances just by riding on wave motion.

The seed was splashing along when it bumped into a boat.
The captain looked up as the nut passed by and said, "Look a coconut float!"

The coconut finally landed on an island, it could no longer wait.
Once it found a good sandy spot, it began to germinate.

Now remember plants need many things like water, air and light.
If they grow too close together, for those things they have to fight.

If seeds did not travel, they couldn't last very long.
But since they are carried, plants can grow to be healthy and strong.

The Numbers on the Bag

From Chapter 2, Soils and Water, page 33

It's time to fertilize,
you've got to realize
that plants need nutrients, too.
You want plants so strong,
it won't be long
before they'll be needing you.

Add nutrients to the soil,
like manure or fertilizer.
You'll learn plants grow better in the rich soil,
now you're a little bit wiser.

When you use fertilizer
you'll have to figure out
what those three numbers printed on the bag
are all about....

Those three numbers side by side
tell you what's in the bag.
Each number means a certain amount
of nutrients to be had.

Nitrogen is the first number,
a nutrient that plants need.
It helps leaves grow strong
and grass grow long and makes plants stay green.

Phosphorus is for all of us,
the second number on the sack.
It helps plants bloom flowers
and make fruit for us to snack.

Potassium gives the plant some
nutrients so roots can grow.
It's the last number on the bag,
something everyone should know.

Plants need these three nutrients,
different plants need different amounts.
The plants won't just stay alive—they will thrive
and when you're gardening that's what counts!

The cycle Song

From Chapter 2, Soils and Water, page 36

The plants in the world just continue to grow,
because of the rain that falls and the water that flows.

The rain from the sky, it never runs out,
the water cycle keeps flowing, just like a water spout.

The cycle keeps us wet, all around the nation,
when the rain falls down, its precipitation.

The rain flows on the soil and ground,
some runs off and some soaks down.
The rain going down is drunk by the roots,
it's carried up to the leaves, the flowers and the fruit.

Once it gets to the leaves, the water starts to fly,
transpiration takes the water from the leaves to the sky.

The water that runs to rivers, oceans and the lakes
doesn't rest for long—there it cannot stay.

It doesn't stop long and take a vacation,
it travels up to the sky—evaporation.

From a liquid to gas and it travels up so high,
then it condenses to a cloud you can see floating by.

Some clouds get so big, they grow gray and tall,
they get so full of water that the rain has to fall.

The rain hits the earth as the water cycle starts again,
life on earth continues as the water cycle spins.

A Fruit's Life Rhyme

From Chapter 6, Fruits and Nuts, page 132

The fruit we get from plants
all start as flowers.
Big or small, short or tall,
all have attracting power.

Flowers attract a visit
from a bird, bug or bee.
They buzz around from flower to flower
all for a nectar fee.

A flower's job is to make a seed
to grow a baby plant.
Without help, it won't do that job,
by itself the flower just can't.

The pollen from the flower
must be carried to a mother.
It takes a bug to move it there,
or a bird, wind or others.

When the pollen gets to the pistil
it can become a brand new seed.
How can the seed find a place to grow?
It becomes animal feed!

Seeds can grow a thick coat,
bright colors, reds and blues.
The color covering those little seeds
is yummy, juicy fruit.

The fruit can get eaten
or just fall to the ground.
Either way it ends up in the soil,
to the new home it's found.

Then it sprouts to become a new plant
and grows a new flower.
Could be big or small, short or tall,
but will have attracting power.

Junk Food Blues

From Chapter 7, Vegetables and Herbs, page 147

I had a big hunger,
wanted a tasty treat.
Grabbed some soda and chips—started to eat.
I ate the whole bag of chips, drank a can of soda, too.
Now I ache somethin' awful—I got the low-down junk food blues.

Chorus:
I'm tired, my stomach hurts, my head and body ache.
I'm eatin' too much junk food, too many fries and sugar flakes.
Now I want some good food—something my body really needs.
Payin' attention to what I eat—each time before I feed.

Now I forgot my own song
when I fixed today's lunch.
I packed some nachos, cookies and candy bar that crunched.
Same thing happened when I ate, 'cause healthy food I did not choose.
I got that achy, tired feelin'—the low-down junk food blues.

I'm tired, my stomach hurts, my head and body ache.
I'm eatin' too much junk food, too many fries and sugar flakes.
Now I want some good food—something my body really needs.
Payin' attention to what I eat—each time before I feed.

Gotta big game today
playing the Mighty Bears.
Eatin' some candy, lots of sugar, my plan to get prepared.
Wanna be fast and win against this other guy named Fred.
But the candy didn't work, I lost, my face is sweaty and red.

I'm tired, my stomach hurts, my head and body ache.
I'm eatin' too much junk food, too many fries and sugar flakes.
Now I want some good food—something my body really needs.
Payin' attention to what I eat—each time before I feed.

The game was over and they had won,
they were happy but I felt sick.
Saw Fred muchin' on some grapes and some orange carrot sticks.
Then I knew it was my fault, I finally got a clue,
'cause all the junk that I ate before, gave me the low-down junk food blues.

Junior Master Gardener Project Team

Lisa A. Whittlesey
JMG State Coordinator, Extension Program Specialist-Horticultural Sciences, The Texas A&M University System

Randy Seagraves
JMG Curriculum Coordinator, Extension Program Specialist-Horticultural Sciences, The Texas A&M University System

Douglas F. Welsh
State Master Gardener Coordinator, Professor and Extension Horticulturist, The Texas A&M University System

Gayle Hall
Associate Professor and Extension 4-H and Youth Development Specialist, The Texas A&M University System

Shelby Touchy
Harris County Pilot Site Coordinator

Jayne M. Zajicek
Professor and Associate Department Head, Horticultural Sciences, Texas A&M University

David C. Hicks
Director of Development, Texas A&M Foundation

Former Executive Director, Texas 4-H Foundation

Junior Master Gardener Publishing Team

Editor: Judy Winn
Professor and Extension Communications Specialist, The Texas A&M University System

Page Designer: Michelle Mikeska
Assistant Graphic Designer and Extension Communications Specialist, The Texas A&M University System

Lead Illustrations: Jackson Price
Communications Specialist, Texas Transportation Institute

Illustrators: Roxy Pike
Former Graphic Designer, The Texas A&M University System

Octavio Tierranegra
Assistant Graphic Designer and Extension Communications Specialist, The Texas A&M University System

Peripheral materials for the Junior Master Gardener program have been developed by Ann Cole, David Lipe and Diane Bowen of Agricultural Communications, The Texas A&M University System.

Authors

Randy Seagraves

Lisa Whittlesey

Cynthia Klemmer, Research Assistant, Department of Horticultural Sciences, Texas A&M University

Carolyn Walton Robinson, Graduate Assistant, Department of Horticultural Sciences, Texas A&M University

Gayle Hall

Shelley Siegenthaler Genzer, Extension Assistant-Horticulture/Better Living for Texans Program, The Texas A&M University System

Cheryl Lewis, Teaching Assistant, Department of Horticultural Sciences, Texas A&M University

Shari Grahmann, student worker

Reviewers

Douglas F. Welsh

Sam Cotner – Head, Department of Horticultural Sciences, Texas A&M University

Joseph Novak – Senior Lecturer, Department of Horticulture, Texas A&M University

Sam E. Feagley – Professor and Extension State Soil Environmental Specialist

Debra B. Reed – Assistant Professor and Extension Nutrition Specialist

Jenna D. Anding – Assistant Professor and Extension Nutrition Specialist

Larry Stein – Professor and Extension Horticulturist

Luis Cisneros – Assistant Professor, Department of Horticultural Sciences, Texas A&M University

Jayne M. Zajicek

Al Wagner – Associate Department Head and Extension Program Leader for Horticultural Sciences

Frank Daniello – Professor and Extension Horticulturist (Vegetables)

John Jackman – Professor and Extension Entomologist

Glen Graves – Master Gardener, Harris County Cylinder Gardening Coordinator

Pete Teel – Professor and Associate Head for Academics, Department of Entomology, Texas A&M University

Cheryl Mapston – District Extension Director, Family and Consumer Sciences

Contributing Photographers

Plant Growth and Development:
University Photographic Services

Soils and Water:
University Photographic Services

Ecology and Environmental Horticulture:
Thomas Eisner, Cornell University
University Photographic Services

Insects and Diseases:
Sam Cotner
Joseph Novak
Texas A&M University Entomology Department
John Jackman
Bastiaan Drees – Professor and Extension Entomology

Pete Teel
Entomology Website –
    http://EntoCentennial.tamu.edu

Landscape Horticulture:
Douglas F. Welsh

Fruits and Nuts:
University Photographic Services

Vegetables and Herbs:
Sam Cotner
Frank Daniello
Joseph Novak
Al Wagner

Life Skills and Exploration:
University Photographic Services

Junior Master Gardener State Steering Committee

Kate Siegal – Youth Volunteer
Cory Wells – Youth Volunteer
Cheryl Supak – Extension Program Leader, Better Living for Texans, Brazos County
Maureen Riebel – Volunteer
Stanley Young – County Extension Agent-Agriculture, Lubbock County
Deborah Benge-Frost – County Extension Agent-Horticulture, Ector County
Bill Kutac – Volunteer
Kim Fuller – Texas Department of Agriculture
Douglas F. Welsh – Professor and Extension Horticulturist
Nancy Wells – Volunteer
Vernon Mullens – Master Gardener, Bexar County
Caren Walton – Bryan Independent School District
Monty Dozier – Extension Program Specialist-Conservation
Debbie Wicke Korenek – Volunteer, Wharton County
Eloise Taylor – Master Gardener, Midland County
Marty Baker – Extension Horticulturist
William Johnson – County Extension Agent-Agriculture, Galveston County
Vince Mannino – County Extension Agent-Horticulture, Jefferson County
Rebecca Parker – County Extension Agent-Agriculture, Denton County
Michael Merchant – Associate Professor and Extension Urban Entomologist
Joanne Witschorke – Agri-Food Masters
Dianna Irvin – Master Gardener, Hopkins County
Darlene Locke – County Extension Agent-Agriculture, Aransas County

Models for Handbook Photographs

Travis Redmond
Matthew Broussard
Patrick Clayton
Yesina Palacios
Megan James
Bobby Malone
Jessica Gold
Kellee Shearer
Alex Sewell
Kristie Sewell

Joyce Johnson
Ann Marie Bettencourt
Deepika Chona
Yvette Esquivel
Bob Esquivel
Octi Esquivel
Kory Davis
Kevin Williams
Taylor Whittlesey

Musical Performances at Pilot Sites

Ruthie Foster – Full Circle Productions
Cyd Cassone – Full Circle Productions
Cheryl Lewis

Pilot Sites

**Southwood Valley
Elementary School
Galaxy Program
(College Station, Texas)**
Starlet Licona – Principal
Sally McKnight – Teacher
Beverly Hetland – Teacher
Gerald McDaniel – Teacher
Mandy Moree – Teacher
Kathy Johnson – Teacher

**Owens Elementary School
Cy-Fair School District
(Houston, TX)**
Melissa Ehrhardt – Principal
Sherri Steed – Teacher
Elizabeth Villareal – Teacher
Sue Cornelius – Volunteer
The Third Grade Team

**Bethune Academy,
(Aldine, Texas)**
Nicole Thompson
Monica Donaldson
C. J. Thompson
Joyce Evans
Merilyn Wylie
Robert Roach
Paulette Dukerich
Meagon Bartley
Daniel Miller
Denise Gaudino
Reba Athey
Anette Easley
Elaine Wilkins
Linda Busch

**El Centro de Corazon
(Houston, Texas)**
Tatiana Guerrero
The Rusk School Health
   Promotion Project
   Mercedes Gonzales
Karen Autrey – Teacher

**West Houston Charter
School
(Houston, Texas)**
Joy Greico – Superintendent

Cloverleaf 4–H Club
Doug Shores – County
   Extension Agent-4-H,
   Harris County

Clerical and Office Support

Gail Griffin – Staff Assistant, Texas 4-H
   Youth Development Foundation
Lenae Huebner – Development Relations
   Coordinator, Mays College of Business
   Former 4-H Executive Secretary
Sue Ferguson – 4-H Staff Assistant

Shawna Faris – Student Worker
Lenora Sebesta – Administrative Assistant
Dorothy See – Administrative Assistant
Myrna Hill – 4-H Administrative Secretary
Judy Bell Woodward – Intern Volunteer
Rita Newman – Intern Volunteer

Special Thanks to

College Station Independent School District, for allowing Randy Seagraves to work
   on this project
Mary Frances Cole, President of the Board of Trustees, Texas 4-H Youth Development
   Foundation
Martha Couch, Professor and Assistant Extension Director for 4-H and Youth
R. Daniel Lineberger, for assisting with the JMG Website design and implementation
Philip Pearce, Executive Director, Texas 4-H Foundation
Martha Cason, Teacher and Master Gardener, Travis County
Bill Adams, County Extension Agent-Horticulture, Harris County
Tom LeRoy, Formerly County Extension Agent-Agriculture, Harris County and currently
   County Extension Agent-Horticulture, Montgomery County
Doris Trotter, Master Gardener, Bexar County
Aggie Master Gardeners
Brazos County Master Gardeners
Harris County Master Gardeners

Funding for this project was received from Houston Endowment, Inc.

ISBN 0-9672990-0-4

Produced by Agricultural Communications,
The Texas A&M University System

Extension publications can be found on the Web at: http://agpublications.tamu.edu

Issued in furtherance of Cooperative Extension Work in Agriculture and Home Economics, Acts of Congress of May 8, 1914, as amended, and June 30, 1914, in cooperation with the United States Department of Agriculture. Chester P. Fehlis, Deputy Director, Texas Agricultural Extension Service, The Texas A&M University System.
4.5 M, Revision   HORT3